To Master Self is to Master Life

To Master Self is to Master Life

Saint Germain

Through the Mediumship

of

Philip Burley

Association for Internal Mastery, Inc.
Scottsdale, Arizona

Cover: Portrait of Saint Germain
by
Nanette Crist Johnson
© 1989
Used by permission

Prints of Saint Germain available from AIM Publishers

For further information on other prints of
the visionary art of Nanette Crist Johnson, please contact:
The Heritage Store, 312 Laskin Rd., Virginia Beach,
VA 23451, 800-726-2232

Cover design and text layout:
Square One Design Inc.
Scottsdale, AZ

Photograph of Philip Burley
Final Focus
Wilmington, DE

Published by:
AIM Publishers
A division of Association for Internal Mastery, Inc.

AIM Publishers, P.O. Box 14196, Scottsdale, AZ 85267-4196

ISBN 1-883389-53-4
Library of Congress Catalog Card Number: 97-073357

First Edition
1 2 3 4 5 6 7 8 9 10

Printed in the United States of America

DEDICATION

I dedicate this book with eternal love and gratitude to my Heavenly Father as He has manifested to me personally and through His multiple expressions in family and friends, both on earth and in spirit, without whom this book would never have been written.

Philip Burley
July 1997

To Sam,

Our dear dear family and friend in a Common Cause from Heaven.

With an eternal love,

Philip

CONTENTS

PART III: SELF-MASTERY

PART IV: THE TRANSFORMATION OF SELF

PART V: GOD, CHRIST, AND SPIRITUAL TRANSFORMATION

PREFACE

Some spirits come back with a special mission to help people on earth. Among these are those guides and helpers who spend long years in establishing communication between the two spheres of existence. Their service is both sacrificial and valuable and it should be treasured, and the hours given to this form of communication regarded as sacred.[1]

White Eagle

The contents of this book were received in 1988. I had been keeping a personal journal for some twenty-five years and these writings emerged as an extension of my regular discipline of recording daily activities, philosophical thoughts, and personal reflections.

As you will read in the *Introduction*, Saint Germain first made himself known to me in 1986. Since that date he had become more and more an integral part of my life and consciousness, and had communicated with me clairvoyantly, clairaudiently, or through written messages. But it was during a writing session on January 10, 1988, that he specifically requested me to sit regularly on Sunday mornings, "before sunrise" to receive his spiritual dictation. I dutifully followed his instructions for the balance of

[1] *Spiritual Unfoldment 1*, The White Eagle Publishing Trust, Liss, Hampshire, England, 1989, pages 46-47. White Eagle was the spirit guide of one of England's consummate mediums, Grace Cooke (now deceased).

that year and was more than richly rewarded by the love and wisdom of his timely and life-changing guidance.

The larger portion of the writings contained in this volume were written as I sat at my desk in my meditation/reading room in West Grove, Pennsylvania. At other times, because of my many travels, I would be in other cities and different surroundings. But wherever I was, Saint Germain and I adapted our means of communication accordingly. In cases where I had no desk at which to write, I would sit either on the floor, propped up against the wall, on the bed, or in a chair.

The time of communication—though most often the quiet early hours before the world awakened—ceased to be important as the months passed. If necessary he would call me at any hour, any day, and pass along what he wanted me to know and record. Sometimes being eager to speak to me, Saint Germain would show up at my bedside and rouse me from sleep at three, four, or five o'clock in the morning. If I were very tired and sensed that my rising was not urgent, I would ask my dear spiritual friend to please come back at a later hour when I was more rested and therefore more prepared to receive from him. He took no offense at this and did as I asked. But, if there were urgency in his voice—as if he couldn't wait to speak to me—I would quickly rise, finding myself suddenly wide awake and ready to take his dictation immediately. On some occasions I would remind him that he was the one in spirit—with perfect memory—and would ask him to "hold the thought" until I rose to receive it at a later hour.

In all cases Saint Germain was the epitome of patience and at no time did he ever rush or push me. Never was he rude or discourteous. He showed only consistent deep respect and unconditional love and concern for my well-being in our working together.

Each dictation, while about two hours long, began shortly after I was in place and had said a prayer, appropriate to the need of the hour. With a tangible touch of electric love, or a vision before my eyes, or the appearance of a ray of white light accompanied by warmth on my right arm and hand, beloved Saint Germain would let me know that he was there. At other times he would simply whisper in my ear, "I am here." And off we would go into lines and pages of writing. Sometimes, he would make no appearance in the room, but rather simply stream his thoughts, suffused with heavenly emotions, through the full array of my spiritual senses. And once into the stream of dictating he would often pace back and forth behind my chair or on occasion he would come around and stand in front of me and to my right and give his words of wisdom. Periodically he would request that I sit in my recliner as he occupied a chair I had placed a few feet in front of me and to my right from which he would speak.

The multiple variations in how this brilliant and benevolent teacher approached our relationship was a part of my overall training in mastering myself and the responsibility of being a bridge between the spiritual and physical worlds. To say that it was a great challenge is an understatement!

When this great spiritual master first began to communicate with me through my writings, I had absolutely no intention of publishing the content. These precious messages were initially dictated to me for *my own* further spiritual awakening and growth. They were also made available to me as a developing, emerging medium in need of a keen and distinct working knowledge of the art of mediumship.

In addition, I was earnestly searching for personal answers to my own life. Each of our sessions was a profoundly intimate experience and not one I thought of readily sharing with anyone.

I considered my conversations with Saint Germain to be private and to me they were sacred, not only because of the content but moreover because of the manner and the setting in which they were conveyed to me. I shed no few tears on many occasions as he spoke to me with such parental love, eloquence, simplicity, and wisdom. He knew how to pierce my heart without hurting me, how to reach my conscience without accusing me or making me feel guilty, when to give me more and when to withhold. He unerringly taught me how to master life by learning how to master my thoughts. He taught me that to master self *is* to master life.

More than ten years have passed since those first precious visitations from Saint Germain in 1986. Some friends and close associates with whom I had shared a very small portion of the writings urged me to publish them. I resisted doing so. To publish them too soon or at all could detract from their real purpose and possibly cause my ego to get in the way. I needed first to apply their contents to my own spiritual transformation. That *was* the original, main purpose of the writings. Considerations for sharing them with the public could come later. Obeying conscience, I have waited to publish them until now.

I am making them available to the public for two reasons: First—as the reader will find in some of the chapters—Saint Germain addresses a wider audience than myself alone; he speaks to the world. Secondly, being cosmic-minded, and a most loving parent and teacher, his words have universal appeal with their divine inspiration, supremely wise counsel, and simple but lofty spiritual truths. The serious seeker of God and His enlightenment will feel at home with Saint Germain and receive significant, personal benefit from his messages. As the writings resoundingly express, Saint Germain does not want anyone to make a god of him. Throughout the writings, he acknowledges only God, the Father, as his ultimate and supreme center and urges the reader to do likewise.

Who is Saint Germain? It is not within the scope of this book to cover comprehensively the personage of Comte de St. Germain or, as he now speaks of himself, Saint Germain. The first and most important reality surrounding him is that he did exist and was of noble birth. Historical records found in museums and in the writings of high-ranking people of his day have established this fact. The records show that he was seen about Europe and in other parts of the world during most of the eighteenth and into the nineteenth century.

His elusive nature created about him no little controversy. Not only was he vague and even evasive about his origins, it appears that he purposely cloaked his life in mystery in order to keep people from completely knowing him.

Above all he was a superior human being—if not, in fact, truly an angel disguised in human form. His supernatural feats of changing base metals into gold, mysteriously removing flaws from precious stones, or simply precipitating gems and diamonds out of the air baffled his contemporaries. His ability simultaneously to write a love letter with one hand and a mystical set of verses with the other was mere child's play compared with his ability to suddenly appear out of nowhere when someone needed him, without being called. At other times, as he walked away from acquaintances he would simply disappear into the air or be gone without ever having left the room by any door or window. It was obvious that all of his demonstrations of transformation through alchemy were but a means to speak a truth: we can all transform our lives through correctly understanding and applying divine spiritual laws.

The "man" never aged. Those knowing him over significant spans of time wrote that he always looked to be in his middle forties. Frederick the Great referred to Saint Germain as "the man who does not die." Not only was he ageless and a man of mystery, he also seemed able to do everything. He was a consummate musician, a great philosopher, a compassionate healer, a superb artist, scientist, and diplomat. All of this won him the historical title, *Wonderman of Europe*.

At times he would go into a complete trance state and upon returning say that he had been visiting on the other side of the world or some other distant place or that he had been communicating with the dead. His knowledge of history was timeless. He knew ancient history as if he had been there, as well as the events happening all over the world of his day.

This is but a sketch of all the available information on Saint Germain. Those interested in knowing more fully and specifically about this illustrious being should avail themselves of the sources listed at the back of this book.

For the purposes of this book, and as an aside from other historical commentary about Saint Germain, I would like to share briefly my own thoughts and feelings as to who he is to me. Many wonderful emotions well up in me when I tune in to my thoughts and feelings about Saint Germain. I have read that some actors are so busy making films and living life that they don't have time even to watch their own movies. In the same way, I truly have had very little time, until now, to think or reflect deeply on my overall work with Saint Germain.

When he is present and speaking through me to a client during a spiritual reading (a phenomenon not covered in this treatise), I am absent and could not repeat what he tells others through me if my life depended on it. However, during these times I can feel his love for others as it comes through me. It is a love so pure, so tender, so caring; exceedingly personal and yet so cosmic, unconditional, and sacrificial. When I come out of trance I often have tears in my eyes even though I don't know what he has said to the client sitting before me. And the client's eyes are often wet with tears as well.

At all times in all places, in channeling through me in whatever form or in visions or in dreams, Saint Germain manifests as a great being of love. And he is wise. He speaks simple but timeless truths and is prophetic to a remarkable degree.

When I reflect in this way about him I am overwhelmed and amazed at the impact of his appearance in my life and of our ministry together in serving others' spiritual needs. He has been a real father and a dear, dear friend whom I can trust with my entire earthly and eternal life. Our closeness at times is such that I cannot tell where I end and he begins, or vice versa. The greatest miracle he has performed in my life is how he has changed my earthly and eternal life for the better. And that is what the content of these writings is all about not only for me but for all who read them.

We are on a journey, you and I. We are traveling in our hearts and minds from darkness to light, from ignorance to enlightenment, from chaos to order, from inner turmoil to peace of mind, and—ultimately—from the physical world to the spiritual world. Our whole existence on this earth is about *becoming.*

Becoming what? We are each already a spirit occupying a body—a body we will one day leave behind as we continue our journey toward the full discovery of our eternal divine self—a self made of pure light. We are *all* searching, groping, reaching, growing, and learning to become whole and one with God.

In the pages that follow, I invite you to go with me, for truth is to be shared. It belongs to everyone. Truth is there even as the sun is always there for everyone, that we may each bask in it, absorb it, and blossom into full spiritual maturity.

INTRODUCTION

Peace will come to the valley of your soul as you ponder and meditate upon our imparted words written here. It is our highest reason to come to earth. All other words, phenomena, and themes are for this one purpose. We can speak no higher. There is no topic equal to or more important than God's existence and God's love. We know factually—not by faith or belief but by direct experience through keen awareness—that this of which we speak is true. Whoever hears it with their heart will know it is true also.

May your life be made happier and more fulfilled by our words. It is our earnest desire and prayer that you realize the truth and value of this writing.

Saint Germain and Band
Through the mediumship of Philip Burley

When Saint Germain made his entrance into my life, I did not know who he was nor was I looking for anyone—either from the spirit world *or* the earth plane—to be my spiritual mentor. Little did I know or even suspect—upon first encountering him—he would become that and more to me.

Though he as a master teacher and I as a medium have worked

together for over a decade, it is not my intention, in these introductory pages, to convey our whole unfolding history. For the purposes of this first volume, *To Master Self Is To Master Life*, I am sharing only that portion of the entire story that is most relevant and helpful in enabling the reader to comprehend both the content of these writings and the spiritual phenomena through which they came into existence.

Someday, when the chronicle of our combined efforts is completely written, it will show clearly and evidentially that our meeting was real—that it was not just mind-stuff, and that the phenomena surrounding our combined mission were carefully and closely orchestrated by God. In a later volume to be entitled *The Golden Path*, the complete story will be told.

The details of how I first heard about Saint Germain are not important. What is important is that I *did* hear about him. It was while attending a healing circle in Wilmington, Delaware, one evening in June 1986 that I heard his name for the first time. However, according to my journal, it was not until August of that year—while reading *Unveiled Mysteries*, authored in the 1930's by Guy W. Ballard—that I became most intrigued by and drawn to this historical figure, spiritual adept, and man of mystery named Saint Germain.

With the obvious intention of giving the reader a vivid portrayal of his dramatic and life-changing experiences with Saint Germain, Mr. Ballard writes in vivid detail about their meetings during August, September, and October of 1930 at Mount Shasta, California.

To be honest, I wondered at first if Ballard had made the whole thing up; it all seemed too fantastic to have actually happened. Parts of the story I definitely did not accept as experientially true or plausible. At the same time, I could not deny that my life experience was limited at best, and that there were many things beyond my present grasp regarding God's miraculous powers. And *something* wonderful which I could not define undeniably stirred inside me as I read the higher spiritual truths communicated to Ballard. Saint Germain's manifestations of other spectacular spiritual feats increased my wish to investigate further. Despite my doubts and questioning there was a familiar ring to Ballard's account, reminiscent of my own spiritual experiences.

You see, I was born with second sight or what is classically called clairvoyance. I knew what it was like to have someone from the spirit world appear to me. It was not a daily experience; nor could I turn it off and on at will. Nevertheless, I too had had such experiences. Reading Ballard's story helped clarify that such spiritual encounters are possible. His book made me feel as if I had finally come home.

"Mother, there was a man standing by my bed talking to me and then he disappeared!" This, my mother said, was what I—as a young child—told her on numerous occasions when she came to wake me up in the morning. And then there was the regular and predictable experience of leaving my body night after night from childhood into my early twenties. I would no sooner get into bed and start drifting off to sleep than I would find myself outside my body. As I looked up I could see the ceiling, and as I looked down I could see the bed. And always to the right of the bed, on the floor, was a rock. It looked to be about ten to twelve inches long and six to eight inches at its widest point. The rock glowed with a supernatural, golden light. The whole room was suffused with its illumination.

As if guided by an invisible force, the rock would grow larger and larger, as I simultaneously rose ever so slowly above my bed. By the time I was floating just a few inches beneath the ceiling, I would look down and see that the rock had grown into a huge boulder filling up half my room. It continued to emanate its golden glow, which by this time had become an almost blinding brilliance, though in no way hurting my eyes.

What happened after this I do not recall. But this identical experience continued to happen frequently throughout my youth. In fact, I then thought everyone left their body at night and saw a glowing rock by their bed. So I never mentioned it to anyone, not even my mother.

Years later I came to realize that the rock was a symbol of God's emerging presence in my life. It was a foreshadowing of things to come. Just as the rock grew larger and came to light up my whole room, so too as I grew into adulthood the Spirit of God would come more and more to illuminate my life with His guidance, love, and grace.

There is much more to tell about my continuing spiritual experiences throughout youth and adult life. But I will not go into them in this writing. It is enough to say that, as I grew older, I gradually awakened fully to my gift of mediumship through formal psychic training with a gifted teacher and service to others, coupled with endless prayers, abundant meditation, and a deep and sincere quest to overcome suffering and to discover my life's purpose.

My encounter with Saint Germain (while reading Ballard's book in early August 1986) had set the stage for opening the next level of his entrance into my life. I must emphasize that I did not focus intensively upon trying to experience Saint Germain on any level, even though Ballard's book had greatly stimulated my curiosity and desire to know more. Living day to day in the "real" world I could not always spare the time and energy away from earthly responsibilities to open and elevate more fully my spiritual awareness, much less seek a personal encounter with this historical man of mystery. But unknown to me, a plan was unfolding that would completely change the course of my life.

According to my journal, on Labor Day, 1986, just three weeks after I had first read Unveiled Mysteries, Vivien (my wife) and I had risen early to pray at 5:00 a.m., as was our spiritual practice to begin the new month. We prayed for half an hour to forty minutes and then we went back to bed. Around 7:00 o'clock Vivien got up and took our three children for a drive in the country. I was not aware of their going out as I was fast asleep.

By my calculations, it was shortly after she left that I was moved from normal sleep to a different level of consciousness in which I was able to communicate readily with the spirit world, an experience I have had numerous times in my life. I then found myself surrounded by a calm sphere of indescribable bliss. The expanse of space around me was filled with a haze of warm, golden light—charged to bursting with love. Though I had not been thinking of him and could not even see him, I clearly detected the presence of Saint Germain.

Remaining in this blissful state, all time was suspended. How long I basked in this love, I do not know; it seemed like an eternity, though in earth time I am sure it was not more than five to ten minutes. Toward the end of this experience, I found myself standing on the crest of a mountain range that was overshadowed by this same unearthly glow of golden light. I then found myself looking at a path made of gold. Though harmless to my eyes, the radiance of the path was almost blinding.

I then heard a calm, fatherly Voice speaking to me out of the surrounding atmosphere. It was not that of Saint Germain. No, it was a different Voice whose commentary was not vague or general. *It* was very direct and specific. And above all, *It* was suffused with an all-encompassing, sublime love that is non-existent on earth. As the Voice spoke, it made me aware that the path before me was a vision symbolizing the course I was called to follow in order to fulfill my purpose on earth.

After the Voice from heaven finished speaking, a long space of silence followed. During this time I studied the pathway very carefully. When the silence was broken, the Voice continued to speak, saying ever so kindly, "All things will work out in your life—*all* of your problems—if you stay on this clearly marked path." It was implied that, conversely, if I did not stay on the path I would not be successful.

Even as the Voice spoke, I *knew* that this was the path of spiritual life and that it was my course to follow in my chosen life work of mysticism and metaphysics in general, and mediumship and teaching spiritual truths specifically. At that moment, as the voice faded from my awareness, I looked down and saw that I was standing at the very beginning of the path. There are no words in any language to describe how compellingly beautiful and inviting it was. And though I could not divine its end, I could see that it continued on for a great distance—a magnificent ribbon of gleaming gold running along the ridge of the mountains until it finally faded out of sight.

Later that morning I wrote in my journal:

The message was cosmic and carried with it the vibrations of healing and an eternal, uplifting quality. I was so struck by the experience, that I found renewed hope in myself and my life's work. Such spiritual experiences contain in their unfolding an emotion, a depth, a "tangible" touch of fourth dimensional knowledge and experience.

As I lay—still in the spirit world dimension, drinking in the lingering spiritual fragrance of the experience with the Voice, whom I finally came to recognize as my Heavenly Father—I became very aware of a *presence* on the left side of the bed. I immediately recognized it as Saint Germain! Gradually I was able to see him clairvoyantly. He was wearing a violet robe. He spoke to me, saying, "Philip, this is Saint Germain, rise and write, for I have something I want to say to you that I will pass on in your writings." At first I hesitated to obey because I did not want to make a mistake by uniting with the wrong spirit world and wind up being dominated or controlled by it. Saint Germain immediately understood my reluctance. He stood waiting very patiently for me to think things through before I responded.

After a short interval he said to me, "Don't you realize that the spirit of all great spirits is one of cooperation?" I pondered his remark and searched my mind concerning all the people I considered great. I was moved by his sincerity and honesty. He exhibited all the hallmarks of greatness in his obvious love, patience, and overall demeanor and wisdom. And who could misinterpret the brilliance of the light around him as less than divine? I realized what he said about great souls was true. Such people do rise above creed and nationality and demonstrate universality. Their concerns are for the world and not for a select few of humanity or one nation. For the sake of the whole they seek cooperation. This realization, combined with the overwhelming heavenly presence of Saint Germain, moved my heart and I got up and went to the dining room table with my journal and pen in hand.

I sat in silence, waiting for him to appear again. In a few moments he manifested to my left, standing in a shimmering ray of white light. He looked like someone standing on a stage, ethereal, but in full bodily form. It seemed as if he were not only lighted from above by the ray of light but illumination appeared all around him as if coming directly from his auric field. Even the area surrounding where he stood was bathed in the white light.

Upon seeing Saint Germain standing there I said to him telepathically, "Saint Germain, I am here and I am ready." He began to speak to me and I heard him as if through a ray of light. Every word was clearly spoken and clearly heard. He spoke to me in this way for about forty-five minutes. Here, in part, is what he said:

The light which you seek is all around you. You are not, I repeat, are not in darkness. You have but to open your "eyes" to see its blinding reality. You are doing that now.

Philip, my dear brother, many things are unfolding for you and are in store. You will not believe them because you will not believe that these things could or would happen to you. Take heart, Philip, there is a plan unfolding at this time—due to God's timetable—that makes it possible for you and others around you to leap across normal time spans and know and do things with a rapidity normally unheard of on earth.

You have a [spiritual] host around you at your beck and call. . . . We here are well aware of your heart, your longing. . . . You will see the unfolding of a marvelous plan before your eyes—take it in stride as it happens. . . . Praise God and His hosts for the work done.

*The Western world is overripe for tying together all that is known and for the final stage of understanding to bring man out of the dark spiritual ages. . . . Be patient, be patient, be patient. Remember always, you are **never** alone. . . . But, remain ever serving and humble to the Source of life—that is the key. Let Him work through you—[with] humility and obedience to His voice. An inner knowingness guarantees safety and success. . . .*

*We are one long chain of workers. Because of us, you are able to know, be, and do today. We, more than you, are anxious to complete this work; for we have endeavored for eons of time to raise man back to his Father, his Creator. It is **all** we know—this work and its accompanying longing makes up the vibration of the fabric of our spiritual garments. In this way we reflect His presence and His will. This is the meaning of the Great White Brotherhood!*

I am yours in the Master and to the glory of the Father,

Saint Germain

After the receiving was over I continued to write in my journal with some follow-up thoughts:

I return to myself with gratitude to Saint Germain. . . . More of this will happen as time unfolds. But, I don't want to create the circumstances for the making of self-fulfilling prophecies. . . . I am always guided by "a will to order." There cannot be just spiritual experiences, there must also be logic and order to them as well. This I always seek innately.

In the early afternoon of that same day the five of us, Vivien, our three teen-age children, and I were on our way to Ephrata, Pennsylvania, and the spiritualist camp of Silverbelle, some fifty miles away. Our purpose was to attend a message service, given by various mediums. When we arrived, all of the sixty to seventy seats were filled except for five chairs side by side in the center of the front row. I couldn't believe it; it was as if Spirit had saved them just for our family. We quickly sat down a few moments before the service began.

The door that opened onto the chapel stage was ajar, through which I could see the visiting medium/minister from Ohio, Reverend Chrisley Witt (now deceased), standing in his soft yellow, white-trimmed vestments, waiting for the right moment to make his entrance. There had been a gathering on Friday evening, August 29, where I had been briefly introduced to Mr. Witt. At that time we shook hands and exchanged cordial greetings. A demonstration of his mediumship on that occasion left no doubt in anyone's mind but that he was good; he was more than good; he was outstanding. What was about to unfold would prove him to be a *superior* medium!

Chrisley, as we came to call him later, finally came out onto the platform and stood at the pulpit. He was *not* there to give a sermon but to give messages from the spirit world. Stepping to one side and away from the pulpit (to our left), Witt scanned the audience seeking whom he was to give a message according to spirit guidance. I don't remember how many messages he gave, if any, before he came to me. I do remember that when he did come to me, he became very serious.

Initially the medium turned his distinguished face away from the congregation so that we were seeing only his left profile. He then closed his eyes, slightly bowed his head and rested his hands—fingers extended—on his chin. It was very obvious, to those of us who had seen this kind of mediumship demonstration before, that Witt was listening very intently to spirit.

After due deliberation he made some initial remarks to validate that he was tuned into the right person, matching up the incoming, spirit world message with the correct audience member. My response let him know that what he was receiving was for me. An uncanny silence and suspense fell over the gathering.

Turning toward me, while keeping his eyes closed he said: "You had an experience this morning very early, did you not?"

At first I thought to myself, "This can't be happening," and then responded by saying, "Yes, I did."

With his eyes closed, Chrisley continued, "Yes, you did. You awakened real early this morning. All of a sudden you woke up."

(I did not wake up suddenly but I was suddenly moved from a state of deep sleep to a state of consciousness where the spirit world could get my attention. I did not argue the finer points of the experience). "Yes, I did," I said matter-of-factly.

Witt opened his eyes and came back with the question (obviously, to let the rest of the members of the audience know the reality of what was happening), "Now you didn't tell me this, did you?"

"No, I did not," I said.

Closing his eyes again—as if to shut out the world to concentrate on the voice of spirit—he went on, exclaiming, "No, you didn't. But you woke up very early and . . . had to get out of the bed and do some writing!"

"That's right," I said, in amazement.

His comeback was, "Is that correct?"

"That's correct," I affirmed with a broad smile on my face.

There was a stir in the audience. This was real life drama! A most exquisite demonstration of spirit communication at its best and at the highest level.

The congregation began to talk among themselves in whispers, waiting to hear the conclusion to this dramatic episode. The atmosphere was electrically charged. I felt like a witness in a courtroom scene from a movie, with the audience waiting breathlessly for the outcome of the trial. You may ask how I can recall all of this. I had my trusty tape recorder running throughout and it caught every word and sound, every audible nuance of the experience. I also have a very good memory for details.

Chrisley was not about to stop. He was on a roll and he was definitely attuned to the powers above. After my, "That's correct," he opened his eyes wide and said, "That's right. And you jumped up and got a pencil and paper." (It was a pen not a pencil—a moot point.)

He settled back into mediumistic reverie and paused for a few moments as he continued to listen to spirit and then said, "Now, as you were writing, you sensed the presence of the person that was doing this."

"Yes."

Not holding back an ounce of confidence he said, "And yet, you doubted a little bit in your mind if that really was the person who wrote through you? Is that right?"

In truth, I did not doubt if it was the person I saw and heard. What the medium picked up was the fact that I doubted *myself* and the content of what Saint Germain had relayed in my writing. But, I did not argue with him and answered, "Yes." Again, it was an unimportant point.

Chrisley, by this time fully into the emotion of the moment said, very dramatically as he turned to face me, "You'd better believe it!

Well, the person who wrote through you was Saint Germain!"

"Oh, bless him!" I exclaimed in awe.

"And you knew that, did you not?" he queried.

"Yes I did!" was all I could say.

In a final dramatic conclusion he challenged me and at the same time congratulated me by saying, "Don't you ever doubt it again!"

There was a stir in the audience as their voices rose in amazement mingled with belief and disbelief. I was so deeply moved and grateful and when it was all over all I could say was, "Oh! Thank you so much. Thank you so much." It was a sensational, evidential confirmation of spirit communication and the beginning of Saint Germain's *direct* emergence into my life.

I know today that it was vital that Saint Germain and I have this initial dramatic and life-changing experience together. It was all planned and orchestrated by him and higher powers. First and most important for me was that this experience established the authenticity of my work, so that I could continue to have confidence in my mediumship and to cooperate and make myself available for further unfolding and heaven's use of me. It was on this foundation, followed by many other spiritual experiences, that Saint Germain eventually came to write much material through me, the first of which is this volume on self-mastery. He has also spoken through me while I am in the semi-trance state to bring helpful and healing words to countless people who have come to me for spiritual readings in the past ten years or whom I picked— as guided by spirit—out of an audience.

Having established this deep and real connection with Saint Germain, I could now enter into my calling with more appreciation and dedication. From that time on I earnestly worked to develop my mediumship. Over the ensuing years I have had innumerable visitations from him. The on-going expansion of our relationship will be more fully explained in another volume.

Relevant to this book is that in early January of 1988 Saint Germain directed me to receive dictation from him every Sunday morning after my customary 5:00 A.M. prayer and meditation time. I took his directive seriously and sat faithfully each week for this purpose, as explained in the Preface. These intimate communications became the highlight of my week. At times, other high-realm spirit beings, including the renowned English medium, William Stainton Moses, and the biblical figure, Saint Paul, would come and impart relevant and beautiful words. Their messages are interspersed among Saint Germain's communications in this book.

To conclude this introduction I wish to state that by no means do I think myself special because of the experiences I have had with spirit or because of the writings I have received therefrom. We are all equal as the children of God. I am no different from any other person, having encountered my share of problems, faults, mistakes, and obstacles and having handled them with varying degrees of success.

Every one of us is a spiritual being and everyone has spiritual abilities, either manifest or latent. Every life is precious to God and each one has a mission, a purpose, a role to fulfill in bringing

His love and light to earth. My particular talent happens to be a sensitivity to spirit and the ability to be a bridge for communication. I use this talent with utmost sincerity and reverence. My heartfelt desire is only to be of help to others.

I know better than anyone that I am still growing, still learning, still overcoming. Attaining spiritual maturity is a lifelong process. We are *all* the sons and daughters of God, but we cannot achieve victory without growth through great spiritual struggle. That is how you and I must climb the mountain of life to victory, to self-mastery.

In conclusion, we can derive great comfort from the words of Sogyal Rinpoche, in his book, *The Tibetan Book of Living and Dying*[2], when he writes:

> *The whole of our life is a teaching of how to uncover that strong goodness, and a training toward realizing it. ...Difficulties and obstacles, if properly understood and used, can often turn out to be an unexpected source of strength. In the biographies of the masters, you will often find that had they not faced difficulties and obstacles, they would not have discovered the strength they needed to rise above them.*

My whole life has been a walk made possible by divine grace. Though filled with mountains and valleys, I have been constantly helped by heaven. Every step of the way my hope has been sustained, my faith enlarged and made stronger. At every turn in the road there has been vision, guidance, protection and comfort. I write these opening words from a heart filled with eternal gratitude to my Heavenly Father, Saint Germain, and all the host of heaven who are in constant attendance to our every need. May you, dear reader, bask in His healing love as you read this book.

[2] *The Tibetan Book of Living and Dying*, Sogyal Rinpoche, Harper Collins, New York, NY, 1993, page 36

Note to the Reader

The communications in this book are compiled by subject matter and not by the date upon which they were received.

While they may be read from beginning to end, these writings may also serve as a resource for devotional study. Each chapter stands on its own so that you may select from the table of contents the topic of current interest that is most relevant to you.

PROLOGUE BY SAINT GERMAIN

THE TIMELESS VALUE OF YOUR WORK

This is not your imagination. You may write. I greet you with an open, happy heart this morning. All that you have prayed I am in "at-one-ment" with. Just know that.

As you approach today's receiving, keep a very calm mind. Do not rush forward. Know that I am in the center of the unfolding of your thoughts. Keep all doubt outside the door of your mind. You are impressed this way. And as I guide you one thought flows into another. If you follow this simple pattern, the thoughts will continue to flow one by one to add up to a complete picture or theme.

Beginnings are Vital: They Determine the Final Outcome

We want to impress you with the historical value of your work and God's work at large today. Always remember that great works start in a small, hidden way. It is the mark of future success of any endeavor on God's part. Hidden away, as a beginning plant beneath the earth, it gathers energy to burst forth toward its highest fulfillment. Its embryonic being contains its full potential, lying dormant in its very existence. At conception, it is what it can't help but become, endowed with all the content of its future self. Beginnings are most important because beginnings condition the final outcome. So laying a foundation in your endeavors is foremost. Do not be discouraged by appearances. Keep on course and you will see the outcome—a beautiful flower! Trust this! As you have been guided step by step, message by message, containing essentially the same input, how can you doubt such an outcome? You must not. God is doing a mighty work within your midst. Now is the season to begin greater activity, a cultivation of that which you planted in past months.

It is spring in your world physically and spiritually. Care for that which you have planted. Know that it rests just beneath the spiritual soil of your land. It is reaching upward more and more, and it will crack the soil as new plants do, pushing the soil aside and stretching out to its full potential. And it *will* bear the seeds that shall, in turn, bear more plants and more seeds. You cannot stop what God has begun!

Pray as you have, and must, to weed out anything that would seek to choke out or stop the inevitable course of what you have begun. But do not focus upon the weeds. Focus upon the plant which you hold in potential before your mind's eye. It is becoming as you imagined—you will see. And it will do more and go further than you have understood.

Trust God Completely and Your Work Shall Prosper

There is a mighty force from heaven itself bombarding your work with the fertilizer of love in every form and this force will not, cannot be stopped. The wheels are in motion and the work will come full circle. You will see and gasp and celebrate in wonder and awe, at what is wrought despite yourself and beyond your control.

Would so much be poured forth and spread so far and have

helped so many in such a short time if it were otherwise, if it were not of God? There is still more help waiting to come forth. Never fear for that. You will see!

Live one day at a time. It is all anyone can do. And as one day unfolds to the next all will be fulfilled and all will be made perfect. Man is foiled again and again by the elements of growth, change, and time. He sees these, especially time, as a hindrance, whereas it is a principle. And when, through trial and error, he comes to see time in positive terms, man can wait with patience through the necessary "time" to complete his heart's desire.

Here, time is not an element as it is there. Why not? Because here there is no distance between two things. Time is relevant to distance. When things are joined by the force of love, there is no distance. There is, however, the principle of obtaining, and this— following the principle of growth—takes time. But we do not realize time here as there. Your world has the same awareness as in ours, that when one waits for love and happiness time can drag. This is true time and a condition within the mind. But where one is totally loved and loves others the same, then he is happy and he forgets time. For him *there is no time.*

So be patient and move within the *timelessness* of heaven, not the *time* of earth. If you do, it is easier for us to work with you.

You have much to do today and we want you to use your energies for that. But we will continue to make this contact. We are always "on call." And whatever you are doing within this day, we are with you because we know you will dedicate every waking minute to His will.

Stay with the course and flow. Things are getting better and better. Think of where you have been, and where you are now!

On standby in Him,

Saint Germain

6:07 A.M.
April 3, 1988
West Grove, Pennsylvania

Part One
Mediumship

CHAPTER ONE

THE INGREDIENTS OF MEDIUMSHIP:
LOVE AND TRUTH

Much can be accomplished in changing one's nature through prayer. Only as heart energy goes out does a stir of the spiritual winds come about. It must create a real whirlwind of vibrations and draw down greater energies.

Saint Germain, I am pondering my situation. Am I in the right place? Am I on track for my life?

"Need you ask that?" *I hear spirit say in my right ear.* "This is Saint Germain."

I want very much to speak to you, Philip, to encourage you. You are in my mind-stream and you sense the heat of my presence to your right. You have wanted to communicate, but could not find the peace inside, the place, nor the time.

I would like you to form the pattern of using Sunday mornings, just before sunrise, as a time to share. We need this now as the work is going to pick up. I want to draw closer to you. We will be entering into closer communion as we have both wanted.

Love Is the Core of Beauty and Harmony

Let your energies flow, Philip, and don't demand perfection of yourself. I have been trying these past weeks to influence this attitude. Many things are imperfect, not ideal. But if you demand external perfection, then we shall never accomplish our goals. *Perfection in love is primary.* Don't concern yourself with any other perfection. As you let go of false standards, our way will become easier and easier.

Take things more in stride. We too like and admire order in things. In fact, our very existence and surroundings are so ordered as to create the most beautiful and perfect harmony. But it is the perfection of inner workings which have congealed to create oneness and harmony, reflecting the order of our love. Love is the core of inner harmony. Love in God first, and in people second, and in self third, and in creation fourth is the proper order of love. This proper order of love is reflected here in our surroundings as concretized, harmonized beauty. No matter how great the beauty, it is resultant, not causative.

On earth you often seek to create the right order externally first and with each other second. People who truly love one another do not stand on formality but upon the conscious and unconscious awareness of the beauty and value of the being enshrined within the body and of the body within its surroundings.

Ask yourself if you would love your parents more or less, depending on their material surroundings. You know it makes no difference. We are aware of balance and of the need to attract people with surrounding beauty and harmony. But it is immaterial for those who truly love. Those who truly love see with their heart and not with their eyes.

Teach the Essence of Love and Truth without Trappings

This period of financial deprivation has been necessary to further eliminate distractions from your circumstances. Meeting souls where you will, you must learn to be undistracted by outer circumstances. Be first moved by us in spirit and through this by the spirits incarnate before you. The soul within the body and its surroundings on earth is your concern. Trappings are a part of all religions, and especially so as they get further and further away from their original impetus. Externals can enhance, but they can also distract and replace. This is your major lesson.

You are learning that in reality you need only your mind connected to spirit to go among people and work; that you don't need all the props of the well-heeled TV minister of today. You paint pictures, make illustrations with words. You create and hold an audience with content and the true drama of spirit-to-spirit communication. (It is this quality and faculty of yours that engages people and that I seek to bring out of you during your public work.) The greatest of teachers and prophets have moved the people to repentance, to reverence, to awe, to worship, by the very nature of God in them manifest in everyday, often homely settings. Why? Because the elixir of true life is the Spirit of God, unadorned by earthly trappings or pretense.

Truth stands by itself, carrying with it intrinsically all the beauty, power, pomp, and circumstance that any manmade cathedral can offer. Truth stands by itself. And so you too must stand by yourself supported by spirit and by the truth that we bring. We do not forbid all physical enhancements; by our prompting we are saying only do not become dependent on ideal physical settings to share or espouse truth. This will hinder you—your work and our work.

Play upon the Heartstrings of People

We said that the more you are your true self the easier it is for us to work with you. By this we mean your *best* true self. Much of what you have been experiencing is for training in this area.

Know that if we see you need something we will doubly impress you and see that you get it. We as a team, as a band, are ever so mindful of all your needs.

Our greatest desire and *the* greatest need is for you to play upon the heartstrings of people. A master musician can create beauty anywhere if he knows his instrument and through his playing brings forth the best sound. As he plays pure, harmonious, balanced music, he rings true and moves the hearts of his audience, whether one or one million.

You get the picture. Study your art—the art of mediumship and all that it promises. Share this art form in helping others to understand their eternal home, how to prepare for it, and how to get there once they have passed beyond earth's spiritual gravity. Awaken their inner awareness with truth from us in the form of practical philosophy, prophecy, reflections on cause and effect in past happenings, and by bringing loved ones and spirit guides through your art. This and this alone is all you need.

A compelling speaker is compelling because he is honest, because he is sincere. He is sincere because he knows the truth of what he speaks, and he knows this truth because he lived it and became it. This is the difference between a charlatan and a true man.

You need not look back over your writings. You can see the truth, know the accuracy and meaning of my words by your own inner realities. It is your sincerity that draws me to you. It is your sincerity that draws you on to higher truth and consequent maintained sincerity. You are a man who searches with his heart and mind to understand life and the things of God. Let this trait flow into all of your expressions, whether giving out or taking in, and you will continue to grow and be led higher and higher.

Intuition Develops as Love Grows

I want to address two other things. Today I shall but touch upon them. Intuition, like all mediumship skills, can be cultivated to perceive vibrations within a certain area of operation or concern. Intuition is the highest form of spiritual awareness. It is knowing without pictures, sounds, or words. It is a knowingness that comes from deep within the heart. It exists because of the depth of love and concern for another.

Often mediums must work outer to inner. In other words, they must start with the gifts of discernment and clairvoyance, then clairaudience, moving on gradually, with higher and higher sensitivity, into the opening of the intuitive faculty. This faculty is opened only when love rules. Love, deep concern, and abiding prayer—spoken or unspoken—for others and their situations, opens this level of mediumship.

Because intuition derives from compassion, empathy, or God's type of love, it is the awareness in which God can most clearly manifest. It is love without apparent form; it knows without reason. Intuition in its highest form is not vague in its apprehension of truth, but is at times frighteningly specific. Intuition sees the Truth behind lesser truths. It is God's viewpoint. It knows because it loves. And it knows that it knows that it knows!

Your Mission Is to Always Represent Truth

To my final point of the day. Be patient in your mediumship— let spirit guide. Those of us whom you now know by experience you can trust. Remain steadfast in your work. Do not let those of lesser experience throw you off by their questioning. And don't give away understanding without others' proper appreciation of what you are sharing. Follow the inner voice of conscience and politely remove yourself when you know that someone is harmful to your work or to your own peace.

Your mission is above persons. You must represent truth and to do this you cannot mix business with pleasure. Though you may not realize it, you are on stage always. How you perform will be criticized or praised according to your adherence to truth. And in the end it is Truth by which you will fulfill your mission and be victorious.

These are not superficial words but *must*—we say *must*—be taken seriously. You can have no favorites; you must be all things to all people to win them to God and not to yourself. We are helping and will continue to help you do so.

Rest now—I am with you always. It is so dear to make this contact and share these relevant messages. Do not get hung up on receiving: hang your heart and mind upon the truth contained herein. Even forget that I, Saint Germain, spoke to you. For I would rather you remember and live the truth far more than remembering me. I am only a means, not the end.

I remain always nearby to help and elevate. At your every beck and call, I am yours.

In Jesus and all the great Masters, I am with you.

Saint Germain

5:46 A.M.
January 10, 1988
West Grove, Pennsylvania

CHAPTER TWO

ROUNDED MEDIUMSHIP:
THE KEYS TO GOOD RECEIVING

We always stand by to serve. We have the desire to serve because of the goal to which you and we aspire. The goal you have in mind is our goal. This goal we share in common more than anything else in our work together.

Important Aspects for Developing Mediumship

We like the fact that you are slowing down in receiving our words, our ideas. Together we need to learn how best to work—at what speed and under what circumstances. Often people idealize becoming mediumistic. There is no one specific path for anyone who endeavors to fulfill this life mission. Each must be patient; each must be consistent; each must be cleansed; each must find his talent.

We from this side have some of the pieces of the puzzle. You have some of the pieces. But as to how all of this fits together we must work, wait, and see. We can see possibilities from this side. We can see general possibilities and potential, specific possibilities. But we must take our time.

The single most important point is our attunement to each other. We have to learn how to reach you. You have to know how to "hear" or experience us. This takes time. This is not unlike a marriage. We have adjustments on both sides. We have the advantage of seeing further than you. We can also see cause and effect more easily from this side. Seeing ahead, we can know more specifically than you how to help you, how to guide you, how to work with you. But it all takes time.

The period of time it takes to become a fully developed medium varies from individual to individual. Some are born mediumistic and still others awaken to and nurture such latent abilities later in life. However, the perfecting of this gift—for all aspirants—takes much time and practice.

God and Spirit World Accessed through Your Divine Mind

Knowingly or unknowingly, you on earth live in two worlds at all times: the inner world of thought and the outer world of physical reality. The seat of divine intelligence does not lie in the physical brain but in the mind, which is infinite and invisible to physical eyes. It is through this aspect—the divine mind—that mediums relate to the spirit world and receive our inspiration. No human being is excluded from receiving our utterances. All do, in varying degrees and ways.

Seldom does any medium begin with spiritual manifestation through physical phenomena. Nearly 100 percent of all mediums start on the mental level. Yours is a mission of mental work with us, and us with you. This takes unique attunement. You cannot be a medium and live in the world in the same way as others. Once you have made the contact, once you have used your gift of sensitivity to reach our world, you are on your way. While many are curious, few really understand. They think they understand, but it is only by experience that anyone can truly understand.

To master juggling two worlds takes time. Everything takes time. For this reason we implore you to be patient. We cannot push this gift. Piano playing is a skill wrought by the interplay between mind and body, often overshadowed by spirit. But piano playing is different in that it is a singular, repetitive effort. While it calls for refined mediumship, it is not the same. Merely running through scales and grasping music theory is not enough to make a supreme musical artist. To receive our influx such a person must be finely attuned and open, but also balanced. Rare are such people. But even they are not the same as a medium in the classical sense. To top it off you in your situation must work through personal difficulties so that you are not emotionally blocked. Emotions stemming from unresolved difficulties block our vibrations. Your personal life must be in order to do the best and highest work. *All* of this takes time.

And who trusts overnight? *No one!* It takes time to trust this mental work. We may be visible or audible to the best clairvoyants, but does appearance or sound alone indicate clearly who we are and where we come from? No! People disguise their real selves on earth and they can do it here too. This does not happen often when a sincere believer remains sincere. The vibration of sincerity will usually protect him if he is not naive at the same time.

To Know Highest Truth Is to Know God

The good medium must allow time for prayer. There are mediums and there are mediums. The best are those who seek the Spirit of God first and us second. Many sincerely religious people never concern themselves with spirits, only with the Spirit of God. They are carefully and often correctly guided, because they seek the highest. Thus they get "the highest." We come in the Spirit of God specifically to carry out His will. He is in us to the degree that we are pure and loving. We are sent to do His work. Since His goal and purpose is also our goal and purpose, there is no difference between His guidance and ours. They are one and the same. Only after we have been tried, and are now trusted, can we contain within us the consciousness of God. We can hear Him, yes; but we know what is right by being totally one with His heart.

My point here is that the foundation of your life as an evolving medium needs to be your relationship with God. You can seek to work with us as much as possible. And we do work with you to the degree that we can. But Heavenly Father and His will is our goal. Unless you and we regularly consult with Him, we may miss our mark. We too must turn our thoughts to the Source. We may dwell in His presence, but we need Him personally also. Each good and truly trusted medium needs contact with Him through personal prayer. We will automatically join you if we are of that level. And we who are speaking to you *are* of that level.

A New Age Medium Must Seek God above All Else

We encourage you to consider patience again and again. Do not push your mediumship. Simply put yourself into situations where you are regularly praying, regularly tuning in. We see from your thought that you think about mediums who seem to be gifted, but spend little time in prayer or inner refinement. Do not compare! Theirs is their mission and yours is yours. Do not try to judge these things by appearances. It is true that there are some mediums who, though immoral, do a fair job. That is none of your business. Your mission is different and heaven demands differently of you.

Such people deal in phenomena and can help others and impress them. They provide a needed and valuable service. Are all piano players virtuosos? No! Should those who are not stop playing? Of course not! Those who stand above the rest are an example to emulate. This is your work. Your work is for this age. You are a *New Age* medium. The New Age begins not with the breakthrough to the spirit world, though this trend is popular. The New Age begins when enough people seek God first and foremost. The breakthrough to spirit world is peripheral—very, very external. The Core of the entire universe, the entire cosmos, must be reached. Then and only then has the New Age begun. Those who achieve this are new people who live in a new way. This is the New Age!!!

Spiritualism Must Awaken People to God

Spiritualism has not reached its zenith. The breakthrough to the spirit world started from external motives on the part of most participants. Few were curious about God. Only the religious minded kept this framework in mind. Most got caught up in phenomena. To fulfill its mission, spiritualism must awaken to the Spirit of God. We must go back home and deal with those on earth and in spirit by teaching them about Him and His will.

Mediumship in its intermediate manifestation will continue to help people further along the path. But it will never again be what it was. That day is fast fading. Yes, spiritual demonstration through physical phenomena will continue, but will be used more and more to give witness to God and His providence. In His mind this has been the purpose of all phenomena: to make clear His existence and His love and His highest will!

As you meditate on this, you will be closely guided to do what is necessary to fulfill this divine mandate. Initially, you *must* continue building a bond with those assigned to you. Right now this is your central work. We are taking this time to explain so that we can cement our relationship more firmly.

Put all concepts out of mind. Do not hold images of what you think must be. Do not base your ideas upon *any* working model. You are being guided to fulfill *your* mission, not another. This is very important.

People Receive from Spirit in Various Ways

We want to bring you back to the work of mediumship specifically. You have been told how to proceed. We are not withholding help, and will not. But certain conditions are to be fulfilled in order to go to the next level. On the foundation of these completed conditions, you will advance.

Though we have covered the territory of "receiving" before in your writings, we will again speak about it. What is it and how do you know? How does anyone know anything except through his senses, including mental, psychic senses? As you write, you wonder. Even after these pages and pages of writings—you still wonder. We expect this.

Content tells you a lot, doesn't it? How could I write or know such and such? How could I write on and on without a break and with unpremeditated continuity? These are telltale signs.

But think further. How do we speak to most souls who are not so-called mediums? We use their thought processes. We come in on their thought wavelength. Do they discern the distinction? No, they do not, because we enter into their thought life at the same rate of vibration as their own thought. To do otherwise would confuse them and, at worst, scare them.

The most important point for humans on earth is that they know what is right, so that they can make the right choices, make the correct turns in the road ahead, so that they can arrive at the correct goal. Do we need to know the *source* of this information so subtly placed in our thoughts, or do we need to hear the truth? By all means, hearing and acting upon the truth are most important.

We do not concern ourselves with authorship. Yes, we yearn to be recognized. We *are* human. Yes, we hurt when we are near a loved one who does not see us and cannot therefore respond to our presence.

We would prefer to have *all* awakened, and awakened to the degree that you are. But it takes time, it takes patience for this breakthrough to come. We do our best, but we must work within the law of being. We must reach people at their level, though at times that may be very low. Still that is the law. Love dictates that we respect those whom we serve and lead them from point A to B to C, and so on according to their degree of love and understanding. It is all very simple.

Fine Tune Your Sensitivity to Perceive Spiritual Truth

But, back to our original point. It is only those who are inclined by heredity to this work that we lead to clearer and closer attunement. Your work—that of a medium—calls for receiving not only information, but authorship as well, where deemed important. We wish and need that a medium be able to hear our voice even within his/her thought. We must raise you to discern the difference between your thought and that of another. Usually we begin, not with discerning tonal difference, but discovering difference in content. Then, as we catch your attention with content, we can lead you on to differentiate our tonal or vibrational quality from your own thought.

So while you now write, what is happening? We touched in with you first this morning to say we wanted to communicate. You pondered and it took time to decide. You thought it was I, Saint Germain, but you did not know absolutely, except former experiences said, "probably, for this is how he has come to me in the past."

You prayed. We tuned in to your all-around vibration. You then began to listen. You didn't listen just with your inner ear, but also with your emotions. You are sensitive in this way and can tell much from your intuition. We had ideas in mind to pass on to you. That is specifically why I called you.

There is a qualitative change in you this morning, as well as a *need* factor on your part and ours. In most missions we do not come in and make ourselves known; it is not necessary. But as a medium, you must be made aware of many things in your work that do not apply to other missions. You need to discern, and perfect this discernment to an art form until you are a "master artist" of this form. This is how we have worked with skilled mediums in the past and this is exactly how we work with you.

Spirit Communication Is a Mutual Learning Experience

Sometimes your mind trails off into material not relevant to our ends. When you trail off, if time and patience have not run out on your side and ours, we lead you back to the most important input of the day.

As you listened this morning, you followed the ideas in your thoughts. From time to time you attempted to tune in to my presence. Sometimes you felt it, sometimes not. At any rate, the ideas continued to flow. And so it is to this very moment.

Is it necessary always to be aware of "me" in these communications? No! In fact, it is difficult to focus on both. Now if you were fully clairvoyant, you could watch my lips move and see me gesticulate. Then you could listen, be aware of my thoughts manifest in words, and see my supporting bodily accompaniment at the same time. But here it is a different story. You have to learn how to receive. You must know me and yourself. I told you that we must meet each other halfway.

Dear Philip, I want to say this: I too long to have direct contact and to clarify a few things. It is much better, but a high price tag is placed upon such direct revelation. Nevertheless, for you we do it readily and gladly because so many are helped by you. We are working on this.

And remember: not all content that comes through just any medium is untainted by the medium's thoughts and personality. So be discerning and know by your heart the specific reality of messages. Spirits are like the medium they work with. Though possibly a little more advanced, they contain some of the same basic flaws in personality as their medium. You are learning well.

We want you to take a break and come back—your energies need replenishing.

Saint Germain:

During your break you thought of just how to lead your life. You must lead it the way that you must lead it. The times dictate different responses. So variations are necessary to accommodate the changes within a day. You have to know that within yourself. Do not feel guilty about needed changes for changing times. Always get back to basics, get on with what *you* know you must do.

About the Spirits Working with You

We want to address spirits of correspondence. Those who are with you are like you for the most part. Their view of life is similar to yours. Nevertheless, because they are in the spirit world they are in advance of you in that they can see many years further into the future than you can. In practical terms, this means that while they relate to you day by day, they are not so concerned about one day on the calendar of life, but rather with leading you through all the days, months, and years of your earthly life so that you attain spiritual maturity and oneness with God.

As your guides work with you, through multiple spiritual phenomena, they too gain knowledge and life experience, enabling them to grow closer to God as well. It is a win/win relationship.

How could we spirits relate to you if we were so very different from you? To begin with, we have our humanity in common. We know what it is like to be on earth. We can, therefore, understand your ups and downs very well and even anticipate their effect upon you. We see ourselves in your life's reality and are quick to empathize and still quicker to act to help you when and where we can.

It is your essential nature that is most like ours. Though our occupational, social, and economic status may differ, our hearts have the same longings and love. It is this essence of soul that we have most in common that draws us to you and binds our lives into one over years of close association.

Often those who are with you have been there since your birth and throughout most of your life's journey. We are there but do not interfere when you exercise your free will. This is your divine right whether you make right or wrong use of this gift. But there are other times, based upon your cumulative spiritual merit, that we can and do help you pass the trials and tests necessary to awaken you to your divinity and liberation.

When you laughed we laughed. When you cried we sought to comfort you. When you hurt we hurt. But in all of your joys and sorrows we remained objective so as to guide you to the correct paths and their ends. If we simply merged into your existence, we would be no different from you and could hardly help you. It is a fine line we walk in spirit, a line between protecting and leaving you on your own.

Because you must become a divine spirit in your own right, we have to discern when to hold on and when to let go, when to give and when to withhold. In all situations you and we are learning together. This is a very brief explanation of spirits who work with you: *spirits of correspondence*.

The Purpose and Goal of Spiritual Practice

You concern yourself with spiritual practices such as certain kinds of prayer, fasting, and religious rituals, valuing consistent adherence to them. We too concern ourselves with these because it is through your consistency in spiritual practices that you grow. However, if such practices become meaningless your spiritual life will not evolve. If you have certain spiritual practices that you have placed upon yourself or had placed upon you by someone else, such as a church, do them only so long as they retain meaning. Loss of meaning is a sign of their obsolescence. External spiritual practices are all means but often wrongly become ends in themselves. Their proper end is continued evolution to higher and higher forms of spiritual practice until one finds himself totally one with God where all is love.

Again, be steadfast and consistent in your spiritual practices and disciplines. Do not flit from this practice to that. Gain what you can gain, learn what you can learn, and then when the time is right move higher on the ladder of spiritual evolution. Ultimately, it is to yourself that you are being true, and to your right to pursue God as you are guided to pursue Him.

To fulfill your mission, you have been inspired to work as you are. Do not dwell on failure. As you have seen, heaven guides as is necessary. Because your mission calls for a broad and deep foundation, then you must be patient. It is what happens in the long run that is important. What others are doing is not of importance to you. Keep your eye upon *your* goals and remain faithful to them. Remember that it is the heart that counts. From this side we see your heart, and as long as that remains fixed upon God and His will, you cannot ultimately fail. Keep on with your spiritual practices and do the best you can, but do not expect absolute perfection; rather, maintain a heart of love. This will protect you against failure even if outward circumstances are amiss.

You Must Get the Whole Picture

We wanted to return to "receiving": But first we want to add that, because you are dedicated, those with you are dedicated. This rule of like attracts like remains constant throughout the world of spirit and between your world and ours. Through circumstances we are all working out our karma.

When receiving, the center of focus moves. That is, we see a complete picture as the center of the focus of our eyes moves from place to place. It is the cumulative information gleaned in scanning the world around us that gives us a complete picture. So too, as you receive spiritually from us, all your sensing faculties are at work moving from places within your mind to other places. Sometimes you hear very clearly just what I am saying. At other times, an unembellished idea flows into your mind. At still other times, you see pictures that give messages. It is this moving about from one sensing aspect of yourself to another that gives a complete picture. Clarity cannot be found in only one focus.

If the eyes do not move, a panorama cannot be printed upon the seeing faculty. So only a portion is seen and things on the edges are blurry. Therefore, you must receive from us in multiple ways, all within your own sensing faculties. Our communication with you is composed of the sum total of sensing. Though intrinsically you know this, you doubt it at times. But doubt is gradually replaced by knowing, by experience.

There may be one sensing area that is for you predominant and it is here that you may most often receive. For example, some receive from the spirit world most frequently by seeing pictures. Still others receive primarily through hearing. There is not a single way, but a variety of possibilities within each person. When one is fully attuned he uses all faculties, just as in the physical body a fully attuned person sees, hears, smells, touches, and tastes. He is then, through all his faculties, fully in touch with the world around him.

Attaining rounded mediumship follows the course of sensing, of learning to tune in through all faculties. It is our job to cultivate sensitivity in all areas. This is what takes time!

We have given a large body of information today. We know you do not want to let go at this time as the energies between us are so good.

Saint Germain

7:30 A.M.
March 7, 1988
West Grove, Pennsylvania

CHAPTER THREE

WILLIAM STAINTON MOSES ON MEDIUMSHIP

This is William Stainton Moses.[3] Greetings from the world of spirit. Your concerns are our concerns, and it is this that brings me to you for your preparation in mediumship.

Today you are pondering the question of precise receiving when you first begin writing. As you well know, I was an expert on this phenomenon. Thus, as I drew near you felt a sensation of pressure on your right hand. This is a sign of my presence, and I come to you to assist in your receiving and with others will help you along the way.

Follow Your Ultimate Destiny with Total Commitment

Your first question is why so many come to you. To answer, you represent a definite breakthrough between our world and yours. You do not represent yourself alone. Myriads of souls gather around you, and that is why mediums say to you that so many are gathered. You see, Philip, each person like you on earth is a beacon of light to us in spirit. We wish to go higher but cannot find people

[3]William Stainton Moses, an Oxford-educated clergyman of Victorian England, was one of the most remarkable mediums of the late 1800's. Although he initially regarded Spiritualism as "trickery and fraud," his thorough investigation of the phenomenon convinced him of its authenticity.

Moses, best known for the gift of automatic or passive writing, received (over an eleven-year period) twenty-four notebooks full of spirit-authored messages, all written in a language of incomparable prose. These writings—later published, in part, as

of this age who can lead us upward in our journey to Ultimate Light. You have been chosen as one in the western world to do so.

Think of your life course. To you and some others, there may be the thought of self-fulfilling prophecy. Think of cause and effect and you will see you have been caused to act as you have. A mission is not a mission until one hears the call—guided by us—and responds 100 percent. When the person on earth becomes totally wrapped up in a work, then and only then is it his mission. Until that time, he can give up. But with total commitment, which means a demonstration of total faith, we can put everything into that soul.

I am not the last you shall hear from, for as your work is broad so shall be the circumference, depth, and diameter of your helpers in the world of spirit. Not all will work directly with you, but some will support in prayer and work with the energies that are a part of your work. Never think you are all alone. Simply do your work and watch it unfold.

There are two aspects to your work. One, you shall demonstrate spiritual existence through your mediumship and this shall expand from where you are now. Secondly, you shall seek to educate numbers of people and bring them to a higher dimension of life, closer and closer to their Creator.

So never think that this internal work is ego-centered. It is true that it is satisfying to your heart; that is obvious from this world and your world. But so is all work meaningful to those who have found their ultimate destiny. This is as it should be.

a book called *Spirit Teachings*—became known as the "bible" of Spiritualism and are preserved at the College of Psychic Studies in London.
Sources:
Mysteries of the Unexplained, The Reader's Digest Association, Inc., NY, © copyright 1982, pages 296-297.
Spirit Teachings, Spiritualist Press, London, England, © copyright 1949, Inside book jacket and page 1.

A Balance of Intellect and Emotion Is Important

The detailed inner work that you do calls for involvement of your emotions and mind, for it is through the combined faculties of reason and feeling that we can manifest ourselves. Today, we work on the reasoning part of who Philip Burley is. We are balancing you, bringing out your mind, your intelligence, which needs to be raised and brought to the foreground. This will balance you. But, through this ongoing interaction, we are increasingly able to enter into your mind and use you for His higher purposes. You are far from a robot or a mere mechanical being that we can turn off and on. We have come to funnel energies from this world to your world. The funnel must fit the need. It must be tailored in size to our needs. It must be clear of any obstacles that block us from coming through as we are.

All of this together is our intent in working so closely with you. It is an adjustment process from your side and from ours. Gradually, step by step, you are approaching the threshold of the door you shall cross into our world, a door by which you and we, through various phenomena, may be able to go back and forth. Today I have come to touch in, yes, but also to answer your questions as they appear to us.

These Writings Will Contribute to Mankind's Awakening

I come to speak of your writings as well. They are precious to the historical unfolding of God's divine awakening of mankind. It has been through His direct revelations to each person and to mankind at large that our Father has revealed Himself, and it has been the handing down of His words as filtered through man by which mankind has been led ever higher and higher. Your words as spoken on this paper shall add to those universal words so as to help Him help others up the eternal ladder of spiritual growth to reach Himself; especially those children who hear His voice through this ray of understanding: the psychic, the mystical, the metaphysical ray.

In addition, I came to speak of automatic writing as spoken about in months past. You are capable of such work. It is your question as to whether it is necessary or not. It is helpful, but should be kept to a minimum at first. We must get into your energies, and it takes time. If you wish to start such contact so we can come through directly, you may. We see within your destiny that it is possible. But meditate, think, and pray first. Come to terms with the idea to see if you are comfortable. You are well prepared because of the scientific, objective mind you maintain toward this work. You have been chosen because of this, but also you have been raised to be objective, so as to be used by spirit.

When you have spent sufficient time reflecting on the possibility, then make your decision. Though you think of this as an entrance into trance work, it is not necessarily the only path if you come totally to accept trance work. Think carefully and prayerfully on all of this and make your choice based upon full awareness of the path you may walk upon.

A Medium Must Live among the People and Serve Them

My life was made rich beyond most because of this gift. It was a lonely path, a path requiring diligence and dedication. But in the end I did not mind. Always, always pray to keep self out of the way and dedicate your work to God's highest purposes. Many are those in this field who were instruments and served with their gift. However, their level of love and understanding confined them and limited what they could receive and give out. It was not always their fault. A medium is a man or woman among humankind—other men and women. The medium must be a person among the people seeking to serve human needs beyond just giving messages. He or she must be well rounded and will thus attract well rounded, balanced people, both on earth and in spirit. Otherwise, the medium may become eccentric and aloof and unable to meet the real needs of those he is meant to serve. Extreme isolation causes obsession in mediums and draws souls to them who lived an isolated life on earth. It is a law of life both here and there.

We in this world are not forever preoccupied with spiritualism. "Spiritualism" is an earthly term that seeks to explain our existence. We are more than anxious to have mankind as a whole understand and know of our existence. But, in spirit we know who and what we are. We have many other activities which cause us to grow, to learn, to be elevated. Plus, such dimensions are means of reviving and refreshing us after a visit to the earth plane. It is not easy for us to come to earth. There are special considerations that you on earth could not be aware of or understand.

However, there are atmospheres and there are atmospheres, depending on the content of the life of those whom we serve. Some people seek the material world at the total destruction of their soul. These are the most difficult people to serve. Dense is the atmosphere around them because they have acquired distasteful habits and repulsive addictions. But, so varied are the atmospheres one cannot categorize them easily.

Then there are still others whose thought life and life activities are wholesome and heaven-bound. Those who serve others unselfishly, sacrificially—their atmosphere is like the fragrance of a perfume, such that one would linger as long as possible to stay with such a person. Few are such souls on earth. The greater part of humanity stands somewhere between these two extremes.

The Most Important Qualities: Love, Service, Understanding

As for balance: continue as you are and enjoy the earthly beauties and spend meaningful time with those whom you love and who love you. Do not stop this. Be normal, be balanced. And then when you draw into the inner sanctuary of your mind and heart, you will bring greater riches for us to come through. Know this is truth of the highest order.

If we were to hire those through whom we work on earth, we would choose those rich in balance; those who love others, serve others, help others sacrificially. And we would want someone of good mind with important knowledge and understanding coupled with a heart to love demonstrated in daily practice. Those who are intellectual only are not moldable to our purposes. Their analytical nature bars the free flow of our energies into their hearts. This does not mean that we disdain them, or that they are not used. But for our purposes they are less usable in classical mediumship to consciously bring spirit to the earth plane.

Draw close to us by continuing as you are. Read us as we touch in, but be a respecter of truth more than of who brings the truth. This is your safeguard against glorifying us or your work and creates an atmosphere that is most pure and easiest for us to come through. This is a rule of thumb for your protection. Now read back over what has been written, and then we shall continue.

Questioning, Trial and Error, Are Part of Your Growth

We wanted you to look back because we know how questioning plagues you. It is less and less so. To the end of their lives, many mediums question. Spirit cannot be captured in a jar, be measured, or be looked at under a microscope. The cumulative experience with the fourth dimension draws one more and more to the conclusion that Spirit World is a reality! But it takes faith of the unusual sort to go this path. It is so much easier to believe in that which you can experience through the physical.

This fact is so true that beginners in this work seek unconsciously to grasp our reality through the physical senses. It is not possible unless we materialize. Rare is this kind of experience and so fleeting that when it does happen people believe it to be a dream or illusion afterwards. This is our sadness, our dilemma.

We want you to know that you have the faculty, which you were born with, to comprehend and experience our reality. And we want to urge you not to doubt. Discern content but never doubt our existence. Question the instruments we must come through, and know they are not always ideal for us, especially to bring pure truth through. Our words are bent and twisted as they stream in through the distortions within the experience of the medium.

We want to make a separate writing on this point later when it is a separate topic and you are ready to receive and understand more clearly: How does the medium affect the inspiration coming through him or her, both in trance and awake?

Continue as you are. Know you are guided closely. Know also that trial and error are a part of this experience. You know this already. It is a scientific, intuitive process and therefore takes time to come through clear and undistorted.

We Lead You to the Highest, by the Highest, for the Highest

To urge you on, we would say to you: Who or what has created the surrounding circumstances that have brought you greater peace than ever before? Who or what has given continuity and clarity as never before? Who or what has brought the connected and interrelated dreams and visions that have led you this far?

Who or what is causing messages from mediums who have read for you to be consistent in content?

Fear not, Philip. You are being led to the Highest by the Highest for the Highest. It is all interrelated. Fear not. You shall see. We are pleased that your doubts and questions are open for all to see. This lends authenticity and objectivity to your work, making our existence and guidance more credible.

Move on in the day and keep your eyes up as well as your chin. See the days unfold and see the pathway open to greater and greater fulfillment and success. Not without a price, but nevertheless fulfilled in His time in His way.

God has been looking and looking for those devoted 24 hours a day to His path. You can be one of them as well as many others, as you seek to bring them up and to the top of the mountain.

On behalf of all those who guide you and stay by you, I remain always at your service to be called night or day.

William Stainton Moses

9:32 A.M.
July 3, 1988
West Grove, Pennsylvania

CHAPTER FOUR

THE USES OF CHANNELING

I am with you 24 earthly hours a day. I stand around you and you can literally feel my energy field. This is proof of my presence. This is Saint Germain. Brother Joseph is with me to assist.

Many mediums could do much better if they were more child-like, unconcerned with others' opinions, and trusting that what they see *is* what they see. We are not out there somewhere and we do not relate or touch in in ways foreign to human sensing.

The Essence of Spiritual Sight Is Understanding

As you saw me in your mind's eye, so I am. While you may see me differently than another, the essence is the same. But this is no different from earth. How any two people see the same person differs. What we are in ourselves, we see in others.

Yes, you did see me pacing and standing behind and around you. And yes, I am in a robe and an apparel you call a cape. And yes, the colors are in the purple/violet family. This is how I am.

The purer the heart the purer the vision. What you see is what I am. Also, the greater the dimension of understanding, the broader your view of my entire being.

We in spirit are not blocked in the spirit world in these things as much as you on earth. We are limited by man's understanding, for understanding is the essence of spiritual sight. The degree of understanding determines the circumference of the vision. The Bible repeatedly speaks on the topic of understanding! And again His word is emphasized as most precious. It is through His words on higher and higher levels that we get greater and broader views of His presence and His will. His word stimulates the mind and opens the windows of inner sight through which man can truly see God and His will as He intended. Who can love as God loves unless he sees as God sees? No one. Our inner illumination by His words brings understanding, and through understanding we grasp the meaning and appreciate love.

Many are those in your earthly existence who have never read but have learned by life experience. Because their life experience has taught them much and given understanding, they are enlightened and can love immensely. So book knowledge alone is not a prerequisite of heavenly knowledge. We lead many by inner vision and earthly experience which together bring elevation.

God and Spirit Guides Speak to You through You

We wanted to touch in on this topic more specifically and personally. You have asked about mediumship and development of the interpenetrating of spirit with the earthly instrument. On earth it is properly referred to as channeling. Traditionally, it has been known as trancing.

First, let us say that phenomena are of no interest to us as an end. They are but means to revealing the very truth of things. Channeling is awakening people but it will not last long unless its content is sufficient in height and depth to continuously draw and hold people.

The masses are drawn to the manifestation of channeling. We want to de-emphasize quantity and emphasize quality. Where there is quantity there is also commercial interest and the phenomena become an end and not a means to higher elevation. It is important for *everyone* to know that he or she is a channel. While an entity may not inhabit your being, God does! And He speaks to you through you and His messages are never boring, nor shallow, nor mundane. And they always lead you—according to your needs, personality, and mission in life—to higher and higher levels of love and truth.

Some of the information spoken through latter-day channelers is but a repeat of what is already known or understood. While satisfying to the curious and to the less spiritually elevated, it is not always universally edifying or relevant. Such material does not sufficiently challenge the listener to become himself a channel for his own divine guidance at the highest level available.

A Truly Holy Man Embodies God's Presence

Channeling has been available throughout human history. Always there have been mediums among you with this gift. In the Far East too such people exist in various levels of influence and importance. But there it is different for it is not commercialized and such people are often endowed with true and elevated understanding, having come from a lineage in which tradition abounds and respect for the divine is spoken and practiced. Such people share their gift in the setting of reverence and strict adherence to a set of practices. They bring in age-old wisdom from extremely high sources, some receiving directly from the Creator Himself. Such people carry authority with them while at the same time diminishing or disregarding their own value.

The guru in the strict tradition of the East is more an example to emulate—not in trappings but in attitude and tradition. He is a holy man whom all can sense and see is holy, around whom people gravitate because he embodies a God presence that is like perfume to the human soul.

There is no tradition like this in the West except among a rare few, isolated individuals. Those who come close to our example are rabbis of the Jewish faith where tradition and living the tradition go hand in hand, where the community of believers surrounds and gravitates naturally and affectionately toward the center of this spiritual resource.

It is this level of channeling with which we of the higher realms concern ourselves. And it is toward this direction that spiritual work on earth is being guided. Confusion reigns with diverse channeling. The value of any message from spirit lies in its degree of unifying capacity.

If channeled messages ultimately foster love, tolerance, and understanding among people of all religious persuasions, it can be said that they are good and from God. Otherwise, channeling can be a mistaken end and not an elevating means.

If the channeling awakens it is helpful. We cannot deny that, in this sense, mass channeling is good. But we pray for souls to progress to deeper and higher knowledge. Poetry, aphorisms, and the like uplift and stimulate, but pure unadorned truth truly helps us to progress higher.

Steps Necessary to Become a Good Channel

As to the practical reality of your channeling, this phenomenon takes place in stages. First, one must have a predisposition for it. He or she must be susceptible to the trance vibration. He or she must be capable of getting out of the way, letting go of ego, and trusting spirit totally.

Secondly, such experiences are best when they happen most naturally in the developing medium. Lower entities can and will disregard courtesies and tradition. They, being selfish to come through and to demonstrate their cleverness, are not concerned about the instrument. There is little or no affection lost. And we must warn the reader that unless undertaken prayerfully and carefully, spiritual obsession and possession can result. You must approach the opening with high regard for your own psyche and body. This is manifest in your inner spiritual practices and life, and in following patiently and humbly to achieve such ends. Always desire to do this work to give the highest truth and to be a humble source for His use. Then you will also protect yourself and draw to yourself the highest and the holiest in spirit. The degree to which you do this is the degree to which you will be successful both on an inner, personal level and on an outer, public level.

Trancing takes place naturally and in stages. Sometimes the first stages must be attained and gone through in faith. Because it is spirit guiding and doing, all things are possible and we would not limit your thinking by saying that there is some exact and consistently precise way in which all of this happens. There are several principles that *must* be observed and there are specific practices that *must* be observed. This is a science and not a chance happening. It is a serious responsibility and not a game simply to feed the ego of the medium by drawing others to him or her.

It is true that some channeling occurs spontaneously, but these are infrequent happenings and are far from desirable. They can be psychically undoing to the receiving soul. True unfolding must take place in stages, step by step.

Saint Germain and Brother Joseph

6:40 A.M.
August 7, 1988
West Grove, Pennsylvania

CHAPTER FIVE

MEDIUMSHIP AND THE INFLUENCE OF SPIRIT

Being a medium is not easy. But neither is being sensitive and struggling randomly easy. It is best to recognize this sensitivity and use it to enhance one's life. It all depends on what we are sensitive to. Sensitivity alone is insufficient to serve as an intermediary between the two worlds of physical and spiritual existence. Much more goes into this position and responsibility. But let us return to the responsibilities and ease or difficulty of this work called mediumship.

How to Enhance Your Spiritual Development

We have touched in of late to speak on this topic of mediumship. A medium is a person standing between the vibrations of the physical and spiritual worlds. They are one world in ultimate reality, which can be fully seen only from this side.

As one who goes between the two aspects of one world, you must be sensitive to both spheres. You must attend to daily physical needs—yours and others. You must attend to spiritual needs by attuning to, and becoming one with, the energies of God and the energies of spirit. This is not easy.

In the physical world you can easily see all that is physical. And you can see facial and bodily expressions. You speak and hear ever so clearly in your world. But as you enter into the finer vibrations of thought and emotion behind what you see and hear on earth, the task of discerning what *is* happening becomes more difficult. Only those who practice dealing daily with humans on an inner level can begin to sense the inner world. And even then it is often through reflection and not by direct realization.

You see through the physical as a reflection, as an indirect expression of inner spiritual reality. Nevertheless, such occupations as photography, art, counseling, and acting all enter more fully into our world than some other occupations on earth. Our effort here is not to make across-the-board generalizations, because man is first spirit, dwelling in a body. Therefore, there is no one who does not detect to some degree the existence of spiritual vibrations—even though such registration is only on the subconscious level.

As Light Is to the Eye, Understanding Is to the Spirit

The medium—a true medium—enters into the world of spirit by degrees of effort and understanding and love. Sensitivity to our world—and we use "our world" only to differentiate—is not mere feeling or tuning in with spiritual senses. On earth you may see something with your eyes but have no awareness of what you see because you have no experience from former contact. Through observation both sight and understanding become clarified.

The spirit world is a vast world; it is endless. To understand even a small portion, and the universal principles by which we and our world operate, to comprehend and work with spirit world energies, takes more than tuning in. For this reason we say to you that what light is to the eye on earth, understanding is to the senses in spirit. If no light reflects from objects about you, you cannot see on earth. It is only as light from outside yourselves reflects from a given object and hits the retina within your eye that you have sight. It is the light and an interior sensing part of the eye that sends vibrations to the brain where intelligence is located. Sight comprises all of this together.

In the spirit world, we can see only what we can understand. It is the light of our understanding that shines upon and reflects back from phenomena, making it possible to observe any persons, objects, or scenes before us. Without the light of understanding we are unable to see anything.

It is the same upon your earth. Though the eye may be whole and healthy, without external light to reflect from surrounding reality you cannot see it. Therefore, as light is to the eyes on earth so understanding (illumination) is to the eyes in the world of spirit. This is why we say that in spirit we see only what we understand. Understanding means knowing the truth about any particular phenomenon. Because all creation, all phenomena, come from God, the truth about all phenomena is known by God.

God's Understanding Must Become Your Understanding

God's presence in us is His mind, which reflects onto our inner sight through which *we* derive understanding. Though we are not aware of it, we see through Him and His sight. His understanding becomes our understanding. In the ultimate meaning of these words, God is omnipresent, omniscient, and omnipotent. There truly is *nothing* new under the sun for God. All knowledge lies with Him and is made available through the minds of those who sincerely and diligently seek that knowledge.

There are degrees of understanding as there are degrees of light. What we understand is our criterion for what we see and experience in *our* world. There is false understanding in degrees as well. On the lowest end of false understanding lie realms you refer to on earth as hell. Here ignorance reigns supreme. That which people are and have believed on earth—even though false—is their surrounding spiritual reality on our side. Their delusion has become their reality until they ascend to higher understanding and thus rise from ignorance into truth!

This is another reason we prompt you to write of the role of a medium and why carrying out this role is not easy. So diverse is the understanding of man on earth as he relates to the spirit world that mediums ascribe a multitude of explanations to spirit world reality. Though they may all peer into the same spirit world, each sees according to his understanding and this leads to diverse interpretations and explanations—sometimes even while viewing the same phenomena. To see is not necessarily to see in reality. Therefore, to be a medium is a most serious and responsible job.

Many have given enlightenment simply about the existence of the spirit world. This has been helpful and important. God has used these general revelations to raise man. But specifics about the world of spirit are often random and even at times contradictory. All is derived from partial understanding or false understanding, and/or true understanding on the part of the medium.

Spirit World Encompasses a Vast Range of Understanding

There are those sensitives who maintain that there is no evil—only ignorance—and that there is no hell, only a need for growth. Whence did they derive such statements? Ignorance has perpetuated many erroneous concepts among mediums. Often it is easier to deny wrong, or ignorance, or evil, than to face it and deal with it. But extreme selfishness manifest in your earth plane is derived from an extreme lack of understanding. In darkness of mind men do foul and selfish deeds. What can be the only true outcome of souls and activities so darkened? Dying in such ignorance, correspondingly extreme darkness surrounds the soul arriving in spirit world. These darkened energies manifest as symbols of his life of debauchery and depravity. Lack of love has created a world in spirit lacking any beauty, warmth, or light. Thus, he sees his own inner being reflected in his spiritual abode.

At the other end of mediumship is the understanding of God and life's purposes. Having limited understanding of God, mostly due to a lack of experience, the medium can perpetuate limited views of God. A popular earthly title for God among metaphysicians is "Infinite Intelligence." That God is! But such a description limits God and limits His access to the hearts of those who hold such coldly objective views of who He is. Then to what degree can such a medium enter into the higher realms, where we all experience that God is first and foremost limitless love, whose presence is a joy? He is indeed all-knowing—as is a set of encyclopedias. But one is hardly emotionally enamored by tomes of learning; nor do we feel affection for knowledge. Only love begets love and only love draws us to another in a way that satisfies the heart of man.

If the truth be known, God is love and truth, or affection and wisdom. We know Him by understanding His will, in divine order. Through this understanding we know His love and come closer to Him in love.

We have expounded on this point because these two extremes of the explanations of the spirit world—from the man in the hell of his own ignorance to the man in the heaven of his own understanding—serve to illustrate the wide, wide range of existence in the spirit world. It is the serious responsibility of the medium to seek only the highest—to strive for ultimate understanding, ultimate Truth.

Mediums Must Seek for Highest Understanding

Mediums must pray diligently and ask always to be led from *all* ignorance to *all* and *total* enlightenment. Such seeking draws to the medium the highest forces to fulfill this prayer. We must fear misleading a soul. We must sow no bad karmic debts, which we must pay for later or which would result in the suffering of anyone taking our messages as gospel.

Up until the dawning of the age we are now in, little has been said universally on the point made in our message today. But we all must be held accountable for our errors of commission and errors of omission. To be alerted in this way is after all an act of love of the highest caliber.

So vast are the needs within the medium's responsibility that neither time nor energy can allow for extensive comment. We will touch in from time to time on this topic of mediumship. Much of this message applies to all humanity, since we are all destined for the world of spirit and need to understand as much as possible at the highest level of truth and love.

Protection from Negative Vibrations Is Vital

We want to close by speaking about the influence of spirits upon the medium. A medium is a medium. His specific role is to bring the presence of spirits and their messages to man on earth to enlighten the understanding and raise up the soul to prepare for arrival in the world of spirit.

Because every person on earth exists as a spirit within a physical body, each dwells consciously and unconsciously in both worlds. The world of pure thought is the world of invisible energy which at the highest end of the spectrum is spiritual energy. So no one is truly exempt from influences of spirit. However, as a role, a mission, a calling, the medium, the spiritualist, the sensitive, is deeply enmeshed with spirit world. His work brings him into daily contact with the spirits of our world. Mediums are opening themselves to influence of all types as they sit so that those on earth may receive messages or information. There are different views and theories among you on earth regarding the impact of these spiritual influences upon your life as mediums. Some think themselves exempt and protected. And they may be. But you as a medium are a point of contact on earth. You are beacons of light of varying degrees of brightness. You draw to yourselves in kind, yes, but as you read for others, they come to you in degrees of enlightenment, and thus each is surrounded by spirits according to this enlightenment. This is not something to fear or be intimidated by, but it is something to consider in protecting yourselves.

Most good mediums are pure in heart and work always to remain free of lower vibrations in thought and feeling. But, too, there are those who do not protect themselves and become doorways for extremes to enter their auras, causing much discontent and unhappiness. It is this person to whom we speak.

Random sensitivity leads to random levels of influence. Are you one who is pleasant and positive in public but descends into anger and ultra-sensitivity in private, or do you have other manifestations of extremes between these two moods of positivity and negativity in life?

Maintain a Life of Prayer, Reverence, and Honesty

Spiritual stability, evenness of mood, consistent pleasantness of character are not maintained without effort. And just because you may give meaningful messages to the public does not mean that you are free to exist without spiritual practices off the stage of public view. Indeed, the higher a medium or anyone would travel toward spiritual maturity, the more he must return again and again to prayer and meditation. Books and classes are not the highest order of knowledge. Most needed for your growth, your sensitivity, your heart, is deep prayer of reverence and honesty.

In prayer and meditation you are endowed with inner understanding of who you are and what you need to do to grow closer and closer to God and to your higher self. Dealing daily with spirit may bring revelations and value to your existence, but only prayer and meditation coupled with your service to your sitters will enable you to reach ever higher and ever broader. There is no other way for one who would aspire to the *highest* use of spirit and God Himself.

This is the day when the highest and purest will manifest in all fields including the metaphysical field. Hear our words of admonishing love and be on your way to your goal of the best for God and humanity!

With love and respect,
Saint Germain and others

5:29 A.M.
October 9, 1988
West Grove, Pennsylvania

Part Two
Spiritual Growth

CHAPTER SIX

FREE WILL AND SPIRITUAL GROWTH

It is a time of emergency. A time to reflect deeply. Don't worry about the author of these thoughts so much as the content. The content will tell the legitimacy of the spirit.

I have called you to write because you are in a time of deep consideration of immediate and future steps. You and we do not want you to repeat, to make errors, in the same areas as in the past. It is not necessary. We cannot, will not, do your work for you. You stand alone when it comes to the soul-center of eternal issues. Know that! These are things for you to consider, to observe, to reflect upon and see against the backdrop of divine will. To know principle is to know divine will. Every one of us stands at crossroads in our life and here we must make eternal decisions. Decisions that can and do affect our entire remaining life course and eternity. It is not truth itself that sets us free. It is our study, understanding, acceptance, and then living of the truth that frees us.

To Have Peace of Mind, Return to God

In their simplistic thinking some people celebrate the truth superficially. This is not possible for you, Philip. You are a way-shower. It is imperative that you seek complete at-one-ment with the truth. You know that; we know that.

You often wait for someone to rescue you from the deep waters of despair. We assist by throwing you the buoy of truth, but *you* must grab it with life-grasping need and hold on until pulled ashore.

It is a hard lesson to learn and obey. Human pride interferes. For this reason you must look past forms and get to essence. We know that these times are very trying. Huge, essential systems of thought are confronting you. It is always the basics underlying these elaborate thought systems that one must return to. One of the most basic is that God is primary. So, returning to God is essential. Even in the midst of your worst fears and insecurities you must trust this principle. Place it all in God's hands. Even if you should die from error or by God's will for higher purposes, still trust Him—place your life stream in Him. It is already in Him—you have but to let Him continue His work with you.

Prayer has always been the most essential way to return to God. Life is thought. Our lives become complicated, confused, and distraught by complicated, confused, distraught thinking. God is simple and returning to Him is always a return to simplicity. This is the secret to overcoming. This is the secret to returning your life, your thought, essentially to peace.

We urged you today to write because you must return to simplicity: to single-minded purpose, to one-pointed thought, to God's simplicity, and then peace will automatically return to your mind and heart.

The Reality and Power of Thought

Man is so ignorant about the reality and power of thought; that each one of us contains a mighty tool or weapon in our mind's energy which we call thought. Every good or bad result started with a good or bad beginning thought. But we run pell-mell on into life, tripping again and again on our predominant thoughts. We become entangled in accumulated thought forms and are caught in a web of mental chaos. Soon we are in despair, trapped in a network of emotions, and fear and despair come to reign supreme.

Our hearts grieve much over this incessant plight of man. Then we from this side must slowly, ever so slowly, work to help our earthly counterparts undo their self-made prisons. This task occupies us more than any other single thing. It is a burden we carry so long as we return to earth to work with man. As we do, we see our own mistakes and how foolish we were on earth—how very ignorant of our own undoing. Seen from here it is all so simple. But there you have created so many false value systems, so many unnecessary accompaniments to life. Man on earth, stripped of all of the unnecessary, excess baggage of thought made manifest in his life stream in mind and body, is a simple and beautiful creature.

If you are to extricate yourself from your complicated thinking, then you must reflect well and deeply upon what we are imparting to you. You rose at our prompting. You know it is a new year, but still old problems from former years arise to stop and stifle you. You and we are most serious to avert such repeats. You can and will gain strength and insight by meditation and prayer. In so doing, we return to simplicity and we seek pure truth. Truth is the end goal of meditation and prayer. Peace is a truth—it is the truth of the state of being when in touch with and moved by the Spirit(s) of God. Living out this peace, this truth, is where most people fail. Determination, singleness of purpose, is not something we can give you. It is by realization of the value and rightness of truth that you gain the necessary conviction by which you become determined. It is by the promise of visions fulfilled, better times, clear conscience, and righteous vigor that conviction is given birth and maintained.

These, my dear man, are not superficial words. These are words of eternity, words that ring true for all men in all ages. These are the words enshrined in heaven. Enshrine them in your head and heart; live them out in your actions.

The End Goal of Meditation and Prayer

Meditation is not an exercise for exercise's sake. Meditation is to gain the deep insight by which to sustain the upward and forward march. The end of meditation is not relaxation, but that these truths might resound more clearly and deeply in your soul so that conviction may be made strong and bold. We draw close for purposes ahead. At any time now we will call you, for you are chosen to fulfill, and not chosen for yourself alone but for yourself and many others. It is imperative that we keep this knowledge, this promise, this mission before your eyes. So whether you live or die, live now with humility to truth, the boldness to live it, and the determination to find and maintain conviction when all others may abandon even the simplest of principles. Go forth and conquer with us. We are always by your side and in your thoughts when you let us be by listening and following your higher thoughts.

You know without titles or names who stand at your side by the truth that we bring. In utter simplicity of thought and love, we remain yours for all victory here and there.

Use Your Free Will to Do God's Will

We told you that we would call at off times. You have been thinking of free will and spirit. You have a will separate from the Father. You do not have to obey the thoughts of your mind. Indeed, often you don't. What compels anyone to follow his thoughts? His belief that it is right or desirable. Lying at the point of a thought's fulfillment is a reality. The vision of that reality causes us to act. But often the end reality is disaster. Even when one knows that, so powerful, so compelling is the vision, he acts anyway. It is then that thought is out of hand. Here lies spirit influence of the lowest demonic kind. Whether blind to consequences or knowing consequences, a driven soul on earth or in spirit is possessed by a vision. Rationality—objectivity expressed in time-consuming reflection—has no place in the life of such a driven soul.

Yes, you have free will. But so do we. It so happens that we of the highest levels have chosen to use our free will to do God's will. In doing so we have been drawn to help other souls overcome the misuse of their free will and unite it with ours which is the Father's. Yet we cannot drive nor compel you. We can only show, hope, and pray.

Find Your Life's Mission

If you ask us to work with you we will. Some of us find those of you on earth who know nothing of us, but are like us. We then work to unite with you and guide you.

In your case, Philip, you have been searching for a long time for fulfillment compatible with your temperament and talents. But, you too, were unwittingly heading in this direction. The combination of these factors—searching and inclination—united to draw us to you, and you to this work. There is a predisposition toward mission from birth. Some find theirs sooner and others later. Many factors go together to determine just how long it will take to come into your own. Sometimes there is a strong disposition toward a mission, but character factors need changing. Or perhaps maturity is yet to dawn and experiences are necessary to raise the awareness and to properly sensitize the emotions. All of this takes time, which luckily we never run out of.

However, it is the end goal that stands out in our mind when guiding an earthly soul. Everything comes together at the right time and in the right way, finally, after effort upon effort to raise and guide the soul to his own mission.

Do you change courses? Yes, sometimes. If the soul does not inherit all that he needs from his ancestry, including, of course, from his parents, then he may suffer, struggling and struggling to find himself. It may never dawn upon such a person that such a thing as mission or life commitment even exists. So how many experiences of learning does he need to awaken to this reality? In some cases, few. In other cases, many. Sometimes an individual may die before awakening to an awareness of mission. Not all have missions in the classical sense. To love others and send them on their way to a greater work than oneself may be a mission in itself. A soul serving in such a way on the earth plane arrives here to serve in this capacity with a number of other souls so that their mission, which is basically to raise others, may continue in a broader capacity.

The Right and Wrong Use of Free Will

Back to free will: we all have free will to fulfill or not to fulfill our mission, whatever that is. To all appearances we can even act in opposition to what is acceptable according to God's will for us. In the end, however, there really is only one will, and life is about learning what the one will is through trial and error and step-by-step learning until we come into complete oneness with that will.

God does not punish us for our disharmony with Him any more than it is God who brings harm to us when we defy the law of gravity by jumping off a five-story building. Our misuse of life's energies—spiritual or physical—will always be met with frustration and failure. It is we who bring harm or pain upon ourselves through disobedience to laws created for our own eternal good. The right use of life's energies brings joy and peace. The wrong use brings sorrow and pain.

There are those who, through the use of free will, trap themselves in pockets of karma until they overcome it. This is the deepest suffering we can encounter. When the soul—in spirit or in your world—regrets his wrong actions, he begins to rise, for repentance shortly follows. For some, learning this lesson takes eons—so great is their misuse of God-given energy and freedom. But, rise they shall if they shed all self-pity and feel instead pity or sorrow for those whom they have hurt in their misuse of life's energy.

When we find those who understand the laws of life, we rush to them. It is a great joy, a great pleasure to work with such souls. They often teach *us*. When we realize that freedom of will means we may choose, of our own free will, to do God's will, creating spontaneity and freedom in love between man and God, we want to get on with it. There should be only one will. It is the freedom to use our energies for Him in the unfettered, spontaneous expression of love that was His goal when creating man.

Heaven was taken by storm when man misused this freedom. You, Philip, still have this free will. We do not force you to rise at odd hours. You have by your prayers and meditations shown your desire to cooperate and thus *allowed* flexible latitude in our service together. We call you at hours when you are most susceptible to receiving—when often the earth is still and your mind at peace. You can turn us away any time—and you have, consciously and unconsciously. We have said that cooperation is the rule of thumb between great souls. We understand, perhaps more than you, your limitations and daily needs. We respect this. You have discerned that at times we are zealous to reach you and you have asked that we wait. That is okay. We are not hurt, because you have done so with respect and kindness. We understand spiritual realities well and we appreciate your needs and freedoms. Because we are in mutual need of growth and understanding, unity through cooperation is a must. We know that you know this.

Be Sensitive to God's Will and Timing

At times earthly time is pressing us to press you to meet deadlines because your part is a part of the greater whole and you must fulfill your portion of responsibility so that the whole will not be lost or delayed. In these times we press you. You are in such a time now and close coordination is necessary. Ultimately, this is why we are taking this time and making this effort to impress you.

You sometimes wonder why things don't go as planned or promised. We, too, are working with unknowns. A variation in these areas—regarding others' free will, including your own—and our timetable is upset and we must rearrange many things, and sometimes everything.

To eliminate any error or misuse of life's precious energies, long for the will of God and it will stand clearly before you with no room for error or doubt. You have principles by which to go. You are ahead of the game and should most clearly know what to do. We understand how confusing it all is at times, but float and stay free in the confusing times—we see you do that now—and you will be okay. Stay serene and calm and patient for us to reveal ourselves and His will.

Your energy is waning. At least you may now better understand us and we you. At the very least you understand free will as it affects you and us, and that is the most important thing.

God bless you.

How Spirits Work with Mediums

You have discerned a truth regarding spirit working with mediums. Our world has been like yours. Orderly where orderly, but terribly disunited among those who have no knowledge of our Father's heart or will.

Mediums are growing people. They range widely from low to high. Likewise, they are assisted by spirits of the same level, especially when working in the conscious state.

I pose the question in your mind, "Is each guide assigned to his particular medium?"

The law of attraction abides. Sometimes it is the individual choosing by what you on earth would call chance happenings. Still others come to their earthly instruments through an organization. There are such organizations here for this purpose and in an orderly fashion assignments are made, though the law of attraction still rules.

Across the world of spirit are spheres or areas containing many counterparts to earthly circles of fellow workers, associations, guilds, unions, churches, and so on. Such churches, such organizations, continue their line of activities in spirit by imparting their practices and traditions in cooperation with those remaining in their former earthly organizations.

Each group, composed of individuals, is no more or no less than what it was on earth. Since free will abounds, some traditions, with little connection to higher reality, may continue in these spheres so long as spiritual law is not violated.

Love of God and People Must Be the Core of Your Work

The work you are doing is at the highest level and is well organized from the center of heaven. Its ultimate practices and goals are to reflect the way of the world as God intended. Yours is a New Age start, rising above organization, culture, and religion. Your work must impart ultimate, God-given, God-maintained principles. All ignorance or falsehood in the area of metaphysics and spiritualism must be replaced with wholesome, pure, eternal understanding and practices. The core of your work must be *love of God and people*—not mere indulgence in phenomena and sensationalism.

You must be patient. Learn your art by practice and by observing and meeting with other genuinely spiritual people. Continue to teach and raise up others in this most holy endeavor. Yours is a long-term labor of love. Prepare your heart for that.

Your guides are of the highest. There are others higher—few—but you could not ask for better. They are devoted to truth and not ego. They will express the purity and wholesomeness you desire in your work. They will always be honest, serving of others, and humble. It is our ongoing understanding that you are our leader, but as a leader you are willing to learn. We appreciate this and always enjoy working with you. You have come a long way. It all happens so subtly that you can't see. But great strides have been made. Much more will come this year.

Be patient with [the new medium]—we will use him to teach you and your class. Know and teach that a medium is human and that until he reaches perfection in loving others, he will indeed manifest imperfection and draw to himself imperfect teachers and guides. This is common sense, but its repeating may give you the patience and compassion to hold back your criticism. Get what you can get. But never fail to love the giver, whoever the instrument, for these are your brothers and sisters in the sphere in which you have been chosen to work.

You need not fear; we *are* guiding. We close by saying that experience upon experience is like another piece to the puzzle put into place. You are getting the complete picture.

Saint Germain and Band

2:14 P.M.
January 11, 1988
West Grove, Pennsylvania

CHAPTER SEVEN

PIONEERING OF SELF

Philip, while you gazed out the window, your mind was in a passive state so that I could touch in with you. I wanted especially to comfort you this morning. I know how you feel and I am not away. I have not simply turned you over to a lesser charge. He is one with me to the extent that he will represent me and pass on my thoughts. Think of him as me if you wish, if it comforts you. Much as Paul and Jesus were one. I will not leave you unattended. Since I am busy I can't always be there to help. Brother Joseph has been working at my side while attending you, though he has only recently taken up the direct responsibility. Trust him as you would me. I shall continue to come. Do not shun him, as he is of me and represents me. You will continue to see and experience me. But as I have told you, truth is the most important thing.

Use Your Understanding of Truth to Free Others

Also, I wanted to confirm your writing this morning. It is true. And it is difficult to accept new things at times even from our level. Your understanding is comprehensive. We want to use your understanding of higher truth to free others in this field as well as ourselves. But knowing and accepting are not the same. Be patient with us also. We have lifted others up for so long that when we meet one who is determined to go the straight path, even to outdo us, we are taken aback. We understand but need our adjustments also.

Know too, Philip, we are limited by time and the instrument we come through. Have you thought that you will be put to the test of your convictions? Unless you are, both by others on earth and by us in spirit, how will you know and how will we know the strength of your endurance—the strength of your determination? If you are convinced then challenge your conviction. If it cannot be disproved, then do not yield unless you alone are satisfied. This is my opinion.

My violet light work has power for some while none for others. The state of mind is affected by what it believes. Belief draws to us those things that we believe in. It is still cause and effect. By believing in and using the violet light, you give animation to such energies and they wash over you, yielding the properties that you need. This is truth, this is fact. But this alone, as you now well know, cannot save man from himself. The higher truth is that man is made whole and purifies himself as he gives love to others and God.

Sometimes Love Is the Best Teacher of Truth

But should I destroy or negate the lesser truth for those who can accept it and use it until they can see higher truth? The great tendency on earth, because you cannot see cause and effect, is for people to rob others of help that may be lesser but is leading them to higher help, higher truth. By being so absolute you deny these souls the opportunity of using their free will and the possibility of gaining future, higher understanding. We must always give love with truth, otherwise we risk alienating those who may not understand or accept our truth but do experience our love. In the end, it may be our love rather than truth which awakens them and leads them higher. Absolutists are not helpful except with other absolutists! How many have claimed the love and truth of Jesus while at the same time condemning those who could not accept him?

It may be temporarily true that someone may not join our ranks. But do we then simply ignore them, making them in the meantime feel awful and lesser? Not if we love as God loves and see as God sees. That non-accepting person is still His son or daughter, still our brother or sister. No, no! No! We must patiently love them, even more than those who may fill the ranks of our faith. This is the heart of God. Without such compassion who could rise from where he is? Patience from our side is our abiding word of faith. Faith and patience are sisters. Faith needs time to work out things. And time needs patience to give space to manifest the calling of faith. If you believe in someone you must not see them just as you see yourself. You must see them as unique with ways of relating to reality different from yours. Then if you believe in them you must love them as God does, not only personally, not only passionately, but all of this over time. Then to let time run its course, you must wait: you—must—be—patient.

Your Foundation Must Be Sound

While you are laying a foundation, you must be acutely aware not to act in haste on anything. This includes judging others too quickly. Watch, listen, and wait for correct and full guidance in taking each step on the path ahead of you. The answers will be there as you need them.

The most important thing is to realize that you *are* laying a foundation. Should you put the best, most tested, strongest materials into a foundation, or something less? The answer is obvious. And not only must it be built with the most ideal materials, it also has to be put together in exactly the right way in order to stand strong and immovable while serving as the underpinning for everything else you shall build upon it.

You are not without wit to choose of free will what you want for your work. You are free to test and test. We do not blame you. Just as long as your testing unmercifully does not become a way of faith. Come eventually to "know" by having known so many times that you don't hesitate to make decisions or pronouncements without forethought. You need to stay close to heaven in prayer and meditation to keep to the course, to more and more trust yourself—know that you are so in touch with heaven and so guided by heaven that major mistakes are just not possible.

You may look back; I want you to ponder in this case. My purpose in coming this morning is different from Sunday receivings. Resume after reading.

Your Spiritual Development Is Primary

As I began to say above, internally, in this beginning you need to work very clearly, very fundamentally. We support this 100 percent. But for the inmost work of spirit communication and spirit use, you must find inner calm, inner peace. You draw to yourself what you are. The pioneer in you, the developer in you, the inventor in you, the leader in you must be balanced with the spiritual sensitivity in you. Your external endeavor to expand the work into the public arena is fairly easy and will bear fruit as a result of your increasing attunement with our world. As we see greater mediumistic capability in you, we will open doors and make available opportunities to use this growing skill in serving the public, both individually and in groups.

So we must admonish you to build the public outreach, yes, but don't neglect the building going on within you and with us who are working with you. Your work with us is primary and the public work secondary. Both are necessary. They serve each other nicely, but first things first. It is through developed and refined mediumship that you can best serve others. By this service your work will grow.

This morning you received two clear impressions and quite accurately so. But think just exactly what state of mind you were in to do so. If you are to receive so clearly, to learn to pick up such energies, such vibrations, then you readily see that it is the meditative state that is required. As you write you are moving quickly—putting down on paper what I stream through your mind. But notice how focused your mind is in order to receive words clearly and rapidly. It is an altered state—a relaxed state, a concentrated state that you enter into in order to receive as clearly and accurately as you do. If you turn to the outer world you lose concentration and this stream of thought, coming to you. So stay this way and keep things flowing as you are.

We have spoken much to you just now. Have faith in it. All truth is within us and we know what is right when we examine our hearts. Whether this is spirit or our own God-presence makes no difference.

A good day to you. We stand by always to serve.

Saint Germain and Brother Joseph

9:02 A.M.
January 27, 1988
West Grove, Pennsylvania

CHAPTER EIGHT

OVERCOMING SPIRITUAL OBSTACLES

It is never an absolute that you come to receive. If you need your rest, you must realize your earthly limitations and take care of and love the body that He has given to you. Yes, it is true that you are also strengthened as you write. When we see that you need extra energies we impart them at once. But there are physical needs that even our energies cannot meet.

Positive Desires and Negative Desires

Desire toward purpose figures greatly in increasing the level of energy. Desire draws energy to you according to the degree of desire. Faith and effort are in the same family as desire. If you want something with all of your heart, that is desire—"wanting with the heart." In wanting it with all of your heart, you shall draw it to you.

When we want mechanically it doesn't work. It is when we *feel* or *see* the reasons we should aim and go for something that desire is enhanced. If we know we should go for something of virtue but lack the desire or conviction to head for it then we must ask: Why? Why, even though I know something is most desirable, most virtuous, can I not obtain it?

There are many reasons why we cannot obtain that which we desire:

1. Perhaps we do not understand the virtuous goal. What is it that we should truly seek? How would I be different if I obtained it?

2. What vision, what *inner* vision do I hold of the goal? Is it vague, misty, distorted? Do I have all the facts? Do I see clearly?

3. There may be opposing images that create a stronger desire. We need to repent from them, even when our heart calls us on to fulfill them. Are they God's goals for man? Are they a part of His principles? If not, then we must not only repent from our misguided, distorted desire, but we must ask His help in ridding ourselves of such desires.

Replacement is vital, however, as we confess, as we repent, as we ask for help to overcome we must help ourselves by replacing our old vision, our misguided desire, with a new vision.

Strive to Reach God, Whatever the Cost

Philip, you already know this technique from hypnosis don't you? We don't ask how or why: we simply visualize while in a relaxed state and the new vision begins to grow and take root. Then as we act upon it realization comes, little by little. This process is used here as well. It takes strong, strong desire to leave the past completely behind—a desire that doesn't care what must be traversed in order to reach the heavenly goal.

4. We must be aware that low spirits are drawn to and become attached to us by our lower desires. Often they keep false visions alive and sap our energy and our consistent desire to reach higher goals. This cannot be tolerated. Such beings rob us of our inheritance. We must again appeal heavenward for the removal of entities sapping our energies. We must know by logic and practice

that they are there. No magic is involved in ridding oneself of them. Humility and more humility toward God is the prerequisite. This together with repentance and visualizing the new God-centered goal are the winning combination.

Many people are humble before God and also repent and repent, but they fail in the third step of visualizing the fulfillment of the goal through God's help. To visualize the fulfillment of the goal is faith in action. Only as we work with and manifest this faith in action can we change ourselves. This is a universal reality, a universal truth. When man is placed in situations where he has no choice but to change—he changes or perishes. It is because of free will that man is deceived and thinks he can do anything because he is free. He steps from one prison cell to another, only momentarily deceived into believing that in his new cell he is free. He is free only when he conforms to universal, eternal truth.

Spiritual Fitness as Important as Physical Fitness

Appearances on earth are very, very deceptive. You have on earth today more false images, more false concepts, than at any time ever in past history. And what is worst is that the masses accept this rubble heap of beliefs as desirable. Yours is a physical culture where every fancy and whim of the physical body is fulfilled; indeed, worship of the flesh today is at an all-time high. We on our plane weep to see this. If the souls of such physically oriented persons were as pure and strong as their bodies, we would have many masters on earth today.

Physical exercise and health are great but not as an end in themselves. They cease to be meaningful or beautiful when spiritual exercise of the mind and the heart is absent. Some argue that it is good discipline to obtain a high level of physical strength. True, but not at the expense of the human heart. Many who are avid fans of physical culture live immorally in their private, hidden lives. They know little or nothing of God or His will. They live momentarily under the illusion that they have value because the body is strong and attractive. It is a delusion of the worst sort. We are healthy here too, but it is because our minds are imbued with the love of God and this love was practiced on earth and here among us. This alone is the source of youth and physical attractiveness here.

If you review these words above you will find them helpful in the next step you are about to take. Trust my words. They are true, pure, and righteous, stemming from age-old wisdom, obtained by many souls of the highest realms. I am sure with closer analysis you can find even more items to enumerate in our list. But for now, this is not my point in stimulating these thoughts.

You must re-think your life, and plan accordingly. The falseness is fading, falling away. You are seeing things more and more as they are. Head toward what you know to be true and trustworthy. Don't ask how, just set your sights upon the goal and we will continue to encourage you. Place all fear and ignorance into our hands and go forth.

Rest now and then move on to your goals for the day. I am being very objective today because it is time for this. Fear nothing, Philip, except your fears. Leave them behind, for they are false and obscure the hidden love God has for you throughout your evolving.

I remain always at your side in all that you do. Know this. This is His love for you within the whole purpose. It is His personal love too, but know it is mostly for those who can be helped through your organization and other unfolding projects.

Saint Germain

5:27 A.M.
February 21, 1988
West Grove, Pennsylvania

CHAPTER NINE

SPIRITUAL ASCENSION:
CLIMBING THE MOUNTAIN OF LIFE

Today *is* a new day. You have discerned well what life is in essence. Sometimes it is difficult to get people to see this. It is not just a state of action, but more importantly a state of *being*, a state of *mind*. Unless we practice the presence of God, we cannot know the blessings of such a life. When our attention is directed mostly outward, we lose the most precious thing of life. We must focus on our real relationship with Him, for through this relationship we find our higher selves through which we can know God. It is in the center of this precious higher self that we find God dwelling. It is not complicated, though various approaches have made it so. Man tends to pride himself in complicating things consciously or unconsciously to make himself look good. This he prefers to standing on the foundation of pure and simple Truth with a capital "T."

The Core of Life Is Man's Relationship with God

To bring those on earth to realize this simple, core truth of existence—that man's relationship with God is at the core of life—is very, very difficult. At times it is impossible. Man is so conditioned to focus on trappings—externals—that he becomes smug and self-satisfied if he merely pays his spiritual dues in tithing and church attendance. Most know the difference between true spirituality and social spirituality. But to step from the status quo and live the life of Christ is almost impossible for most. So we and they suffer. We have often abandoned great plans for such people in the sense that we place little hope in their usefulness for God's central and sublime calling. So we start working from youth. Even if this takes longer in raising from that level, still the end will be what is most desirable to God. We need the pure in heart to save the world.

So, Philip, we want you to continue to look internally, at essence and not appearances, at motives and not merely actions. These things will reveal themselves to you and yours if—as you have prayed—you remain humble. *All* of the answers will come—guaranteed!

Today is going to be a beautiful day internally for you and your family. You are coming into that realization we have wanted for you as we know this is the center of restoration of the human soul: man in his distorted nature is greedy. He wants all knowledge, he wants to know everything, while at the same time he has not made use of what has already been given. He becomes a thief of truth: he would rob the coffers of heaven, storing up what is taken to appear wise—and still he seeks for more. Such a person has not learned even the rudimentary laws of life. But if he or she will begin the process of submission by confession—an admission of his true need of God as the source of all life—areas that are presently closed will open, and he will see life as it is. He then can come into harmony with life and begin to grow, to change.

Everyone is looking for the panacea, the golden chalice. It lies within. Remember, he who finds the Holy Grail is he who is most pure. The purity of self leads one by inner recognition to the purity within the Holy Grail. This and this alone is the object lesson of that classical story. We cannot trick God into favoring us. We cannot curry His favor to merely wink at our shortcomings. We begin the ascent with humility. Humility increasingly emerges as we realize where life, where love, where wisdom come from. Give me a man who truly knows God by experience and who through experience has obtained true humility, and I will show you a man on the edge of his divine, highest self. It is so simple.

Relationship of the Creator to the Created

All of my efforts have been to illustrate this central point. I cannot take credit for it. It is intrinsic to the creation of all things: "That which is created must be grateful to that which created it." There can be no other result from higher to lower creation. We have come to understand this by our life on earth and since coming to "this world." Here such a principle of Creator to the created is obvious. There is no sense here of slavish obedience and placating or appeasing God. No, it is seen clearly that *all things* have come from Him. We do not express our thanks out of obligation, but out of pure recognition that He created all. We not only respect this and are filled with gratitude, but we see and experience the divine love out of which He created all. This love of His overwhelms us. We are moved not only by His impulse to create us, but also by the reality of that love that is here apparent everywhere. There is no sense of obligation. Rather, because we can know here by firsthand, ongoing experience, we have no reason to think or feel otherwise. We love because He loved—and loves—us. The air is the electricity of His love that gives us life. We bask in it! There are no exceptions to this principle. Unless one can detect His reality, he will not be at home in these rarefied realms and will have to occupy a lesser realm, where he may know God only by reflection, and not by a direct emanation of His ever-abiding love.

I could portray reams of truth through you, Philip. But it is not my role simply to give you, and others through you, a stockpile of truth for you to sort through. I told you before that we come to bring truth. But we give more and higher truth when we discern your grasp and actual practice of what has already been given. Anything else would over-stimulate your mental faculties, leaving your heart lagging behind.

Climb the Spiritual Mountain of Life to Reach God

Of course, we may give morsels of further truth to entice you to go on or hope for what is to come. But a full menu of truth is seldom given—it is more like giving courses in a meal. Finish one course in both understanding and living and the next course will be served. This is the law of life. If one is not growing, is not realizing progress, he should ask himself if he has practiced in life what he has already been given in intellect. Does he live what he knows to be true? Does he know truth and preach it, but not live it? If in any case he does not live the truth he has been given, then he shall not obtain more from us. He may be encouraged with multiple expressions of the same truth, but he will not be given higher truth. It is the law of life. Can anyone pass from the base of a mountain to the peak without passing over all that is between the base and the peak? Impossible! And so you cannot arrive here in the highest of highest abodes without climbing the mountain of life. Everything that abides there abides here.

We would say, as so many have said, that it may be better to put away all that we have and all that we are and bow before the eternal reality of God. Start, my beloved ones, at the base of the Mountain of God. Start at the bottom or start in other words in the state of extreme humility before the Mountain of Life. Keep this image ever before you as you pray each day. This is your safety net for ascending.

The Ascended Masters Are Your Example

We have been labeled Ascended Masters. We laugh from this side at the various and multiple concepts you earthlings have of this lofty title. We are not flattered. If we are ascended, it is the Mountain of Life that we ascended. This in itself should tell you the nature of our ascent. We are not celestial beings raised from humanity by any other means but by the springboard effect of humility. We practiced, through much trial and error, the presence of God. We stumbled much to find the key. We came to realize that we exist, because He exists. And this humbled us so greatly that we forsook our previous ideas of life and self and committed our lives to humility before this great principle, this great "I AM," this ever-loving, ever-giving, eternal, glorious, sensitive, tender being whom we call God, and personally, our Father. This is the road of an ascended master.

And so you see, we have scaled the heights and plumbed the craggy depths of life's mountainside. And from this side we continued our climb with helping others up this undeniable Mountain of Life. We have climbed many paths and many cliffs, many sharp and jagged ways, in helping others up this mountain. We have repeated, thousands and thousands and thousands of times, the same truths. One of the most repeated truths we have whispered in countless, countless spiritual ears is, "You can do it!"

God and Spirit Guides Eager to Assist Your Climb

We deliver this message today for its content alone, to inspire others to humble themselves and discover the hidden manna in the craggy rocks at the base of the Mountain of Life. We want to dispel the metaphysical mumbo-jumbo surrounding today's teachings about the ascended masters. See the mountain ahead and above you and begin your climb. On the way up you shall meet us, but we will not be ensconced on thrones. No, you will see us working there on the mountainside beside you and millions of other souls ascending those often steep and overwhelming slopes.

And we shall learn together how to conquer the mountain called Life. And one day, when you have carved a trail for others and yourself to the top, you will rest only a short while before you begin your *descent* back down to bring others up. For while you may bask in the total love and understanding of God at the top, you will discover that He is not truly there but on the *mountainsides*, at all levels, pulling, pushing, beseeching, praying, and crying.

He cannot rest at the top. He in all His love for His children is compelled by love's nature to save that which He bore. He, my dearly beloved children, is the victim of His own love! And so will you be if you love enough! In this love there is no such thing as too tired, too hungry, too lonely. Being who and what he is and was, Jesus said, "I must be about my Father's business." Love's call made Jesus that way.

We must all be about our Father's business.

In Him and His mighty love,

Saint Germain and All

5:39 A.M.
March 6, 1988
West Grove, Pennsylvania

CHAPTER TEN

BELIEVE IN YOURSELF

Guides are guides, and we will help you master your circumstances as we are and have been doing. All is within God's hands and time.

Have Faith in God's Guidance and Timing

The single most important point in this writing is your connection to me. It is for this inner reason that we need constantly to be close. If you had no one to turn to but these writings, this guidance, pouring through you from those who guide you in spirit, it would suffice. And you must get to this level of confidence, not only in our guidance and purpose, but also in your ability to receive correctly. This is all coming with time. Little by little, doubt of us and yourself is fading. Because none of us can see ourselves objectively, we cannot see our own progress. And you *are* making progress. Do not push things. Always remember, everything in *divine order*. You are not to be merely a medium between our side of the cosmos and your side. Your mission is larger, more expansive, more encompassing.

As to others whom you trust and believe in, mark well in your mind as I have told you in the past. Do not believe in anyone or anything; that is, those things that are supposed to be, will happen at God's prompting. You cannot force things. You are disappointed in someone, in several. Don't take it personally. There are reasons beyond your concern or for these things happening as they do. Doors will open where they will, and as they are supposed to. And don't fear others. You have a strong tendency to put others up and yourself down. Take a step up—love and believe in yourself!

We don't want you to develop a fatalistic point of view in your life, but rather, a realistic attitude toward other people's responses. You cannot live dependent upon others' reactions and be a leader. If you know what is right, both according to divine law and your mission, then you must do it regardless of others' thoughts. You are guided by us for a specific work in a specific way.

Fulfill Your Mission by Mastering Love

Do not constrain yourself under the pressure of what others think. You cannot expect others always to understand, agree, or follow. Some will, some won't. To be a leader, you need clearly to make courageous decisions based upon your belief in Him and His will, and not upon the whim, ideas, or concepts of others. This does not mean that He doesn't speak through others to you. Always listen for His guidance through even seemingly insignificant souls. But do not worship anyone, including me, who guides you. Only He is worthy of such attention.

Continue to love others who are guided your way for specific purposes. Love them as yourself. Does this sound familiar? Pray for them and trust us to guide those who are to be of value to your work, to be inspired to help in the way that they can help. None of us can grow in isolation. We cannot use people merely as stepping stones. Love is the pathway to God—mission is secondary. And if you will master loving correctly, you will fulfill your mission. Respect others' needs to do what they have to do, and it will follow that they will come to respect you. If you see the best in others, they—by the law of returning reciprocal energy—will see the best in you.

We do not mean that you should be without concept or convictions. Be absolute where you know only one thing is acceptable. But be discerning as to just how you dispense your life's energy. Never exhibit hostility or judgment. The only exception is when you have loved to such a degree that another will know your momentary strong words are founded upon the love you have totally invested in them. This is the center of correct, heavenly parenting. A parent must not only discipline with objective truth, but must love in word and deed. Without this balance you will not be successful.

Have Faith in Yourself, God Is Always with You

Doors will open as they will open. When the time is right things will unfold as they were meant to. But unless we remain connected and in "at-one-ment," we may not discern fully or correctly. This does not mean you must always rush to write in order to receive guidance. We would not have that either. You must have confidence in your own feeling, and reasoning capacities beyond us, based upon the truth you know. You will stand alone, apart from us, to be allowed to become your own unique, confident self. Not all is spirit. Free will and the nature of each soul demands we stand as individuals from time to time to become our full, confident, perfected selves.

If you must run to us for every answer you cannot grow in your own capacity to discern, to build your own personal, individualized relationship with Him.

There is *no* time in which anyone of us stands truly alone because we are always in His energy of love. But as we make ourselves ever more available to Him, it becomes automatic for His energy in all forms to flow into the vacuum of our neediness and to complete our thoughts and feelings.

You need us as His representatives, yes. And you need us in this mission of mediumship, for it is through this connection that you and we fulfill the divine calling. This connection to us is the base of the fulfillment of this work. Without it, the work cannot be accomplished.

Move on into the day. Be strong in yourself, believe in yourself, and become your Divine Self! He in you and you in Him, through which you can and will fulfill the highest level of true divine mediumship.

Always at your side for His purposes,
Saint Germain and All

6:12 A.M.
April 9, 1988
West Grove, Pennsylvania

Part Three
Self-Mastery

CHAPTER ELEVEN

THE WAY OF SELF-MASTERY

I wanted to come to you while the day was still young. Pray first to attune more and then we shall begin.

We feel the yearning of your heart. It is a sign of freedoms to come. We urge you to go forth as you have been thinking. If you take personal responsibility for your life space, it will be another step toward growing emotional and mental stability. In your inner self you are very stable. It is in your outer mind that you struggle. You will not become more free and more stable through others but through your relationship with Him. Many make this mistake of making gods of men. No man or woman is truly stable without a true, ongoing relationship with the Father.

The Hallmark of Divinity: Love and Service

It is best to be near those who are most holy. It is best to surround yourself with such individuals. Seek for such serious people and they will be drawn to you. It takes the right inherited heart and much time to cultivate such a character.

Holy has nothing to do with trappings but rather to do with character. Just how devout are they in their daily attendance of God? How much do they seek to comfort and help others? How happy or peaceful are they deep inside? How many tears do they shed for heaven and humanity? How much do they seek to come closer to God? These are hallmarks of divinity.

Jesus' entire life was consumed in caring for and loving others at the sacrifice of himself. His inborn sensitivity enabled him to experience God from the most minute to the cosmic level. This intuitive ability was greatly enhanced and fine tuned through the suffering he encountered as he sought to do God's will without reservation. Let us emulate Jesus if we want to achieve true holiness and obtain spiritual maturity.

We cannot truly judge another. We do not stand within his heart and mind to know what underlies a person's acts. Even outward signs are not always evidence of inner rumblings or activity. Only God can discern, for He, dwelling within His child, knows the inner secrets of motive, of longing, of thoughts that are constructive or destructive. We need always to draw near the Most High because He is the source of *all* life and has therefore all the answers. It is foolish to consult with or believe in man or in ourselves *alone*. But many do. Here we err greatly! Trust no one but God to be your confidant—not even me. Only He can truly lead from deep, deep within your soul where lie the strings of character to be played upon by Him. We cannot stress this point enough. Only when we are fully stoked with the fuel of God can we trust ourselves to discern man.

Integrity Comes by Always Seeking God's Will

You will learn much from these recent happenings. Be secure in God; it is He who guides you in all ways. And the more you consult Him, the more and closer He can guide. Unless we go to Him and repeatedly ask, we do not learn the secret strength that is derived from that relationship. It is the only relationship that is truly reliable 100 percent of the time. God is unchanging. Without

Him humans have no integrity, and change rapidly.

He provides the only real, ultimate direction in life. One is truly free only in Him. And character remains steady only when we remain always with Him. Master this relationship and you will master all lesser relationships. Do not fear man—fear God! That is, respect God above all. And lead others to this same awareness and practice. And again, as we have said before, then you cannot fail!

Let more time pass to make your great decisions. We need that time to impress you. Let *no one* pressure you to hasty decisions in large matters. We see your fear of being or appearing self-righteous or spiritually aloof. This will never happen if you sincerely remain friends with Almighty God. Never! Self-righteousness comes from thinking oneself the center of all knowledge and all goodness. No, staying with Him lets us know where "it all" comes from. And in this we can't go wrong.

Self-mastery at its peak is mastery of the self in God. Man is created so that as he aligns himself with God he obtains His strength, His wisdom, His character. Remember too, that when such a person appears to men, he is often an affront to their unrighteousness and is rejected. This is part of what you are experiencing presently. But the only salve to rub on the situation is the love of God. So go to Him as the container of this love and be healed, and gather there the salve of love that you can take to others. Remember, too, while we sow and reap and do so earnestly and with all self-sacrifice, it is we who benefit the most. We do not do it for this reason, but these are the results nevertheless.

Be a Wayshower, a Giver of Truth

I want to address what you were just reflecting upon: you think of another with whom you feel uncomfortable. You may, or may not, be right. But, it is not your job to judge them. It is your responsibility to uphold the example of love and faith on all levels. Do not expect to feel one with all. Your responsibility is to meet spiritual needs in a specific way. While you may be concerned about them, it is not your responsibility to play God over any aspect of their life. Not at all! We are not with you for this. Your primary work is that of way-shower and giver of truth through your mediumship. As we have said, that is enough. If they will follow your words, example and messages, they will be significantly helped.

Everyone has the same opportunity to develop, to spend time with their spirit force as you do. But, most do not do so. There are many reasons. They get what they can get and go on their way. It is not all predestined whether one does any particular mission. There are many factors involved, not the least of which is self-motivation. Man in his free will is not guided in every word, in every decision. He must become a person in himself. His personhood must lead him to where he needs to go. Some must struggle with this until, by trial and error, they discover their own need for self-mastery of the energies which He has allowed them.

Unfortunately, most tire along the way and easily become bored searching for new stimulation, new thrills. But, it is the inner man that must respond and feel compelled to do what is necessary to arrive safely at heaven's door. Most do not want to do that. So do not expect miracles or great, great responses. Maybe one in one hundred is really and truly ready for this calling. But none of this is said in condemnation. We mention it to put your life and perspective in order, so that you will not be dismayed. Be excited about the possibilities in your life, and long to share them to help others. But do not expect that every seed your efforts fall upon will grow, and, if they do, that each will be like you. Some have other ultimate work to do. Still others do not respond because they are not yet even awakened!

Consciously Appeal to the Positive under All Conditions

Believe in yourself! You have unique value, certain spiritual strengths, and a track record of good deeds, having helped others more than you are aware. There will be those who will criticize you. We do not say not to listen, not to be open or vulnerable, but do not take any and all criticism or advice seriously. Ask yourself always: is it true and is it given in the spirit of love? Be discerning. Accept what is true, take responsibility and then turn it over to God. Because what you are doing is important, heaven is eager to support you. Not just you, but all utterly serious workers in His vineyard. You are one of them and you must take your calling seriously.

Remember to keep your own heart clear of all negativity. You cannot determine another's life. Only your own. Others must make their own decisions and go through the pain of wrong decisions. You are ahead of those whom you lead; if not, you could not lead. Stifle your present negative period with diversion and in loving others as you would want to be loved.

We do not say you are without fault, nor would we pamper you or protect you from the reality of what is right and true. But, we want to emphasize positive thoughts and positive directions, for ultimately these are the only things that solve life's problems. You especially have been prone to look back. What for? There is nothing back there. Move on in positivity. See good in each person and each situation. Consciously appeal to that in yourself and others.

You Are Being Specifically Guided to Your Goal

Yes, others want to pull you down to their level of life. We will not have this. You are not wrong in your inner voice, but you must handle it wisely. The lesser things must serve the higher things. Such order is apparent in creation. The physical must serve the spiritual. Be leery of those who tell you they want to correct you, if they do not come in love. Such lesser energy destroys the soul. However, be careful too that in *your* life you truly serve the greater.

These days will pass quickly away as new awareness comes to mind. Look to that as you are being very specifically guided to your goal. There are those who work externally and note little change inwardly. But with you, not only are you growing mentally, we are busily refining your spiritual energies to prepare you as an instrument. This you know and will see more and more clearly as the weeks and months unfold. It is a precise and exacting work. Know that you are increasingly attuned to be sensitive. This will make it harder to be close to those who are not clear, whose motives are lesser.

Draw into yourself and protect yourself. But do not be retiring or a recluse with this sensitivity. Rather, protect your own openness by giving out positively to others, whether you feel like it or not. It is not they whom you must protect in this case, but yourself. This is not selfish; it goes with the territory. *Everyone* should strive to be positive, to keep their own vibrations clear of negative interference. It is wise and necessary. Do not expect others to do this for you.

It is a good day, Philip, to set your feet on the track of progress. In this way the tarnished dream will shine again and the vision to advance will appear. And you *will* go on. No one can destroy or defeat this work set in motion. Look up and not down, look forward and not backward. Love yourself by staying close to Him.

Saint Germain

7:52 A.M.
April 22, 1988
West Grove, Pennsylvania

Chapter Twelve

The Ultimate Purpose of Positive Thinking

As you look at humanity, as you touch the inner lives of people, what do you find? There is little perfection. Whom do you know who is not struggling? This is not said to justify anything. It is said to put your life in perspective. You must *not* condemn yourself for failure. You must encourage yourself for success.

Meet People Where They Are on Their Spiritual Path

We do not withdraw our love, our compassion. We may step aside as you exercise free will and we may suffer should you misuse it. But we do not condemn! Reformation takes place every day in souls formerly thought to be lost to reformation. Because His force and forces are ever at work in the minds and hearts of mankind, both in the spirit world and here on earth, evolution continually unfolds. We meet people where they are. Not everyone is ready for the higher causes you seek. Each individual must be allowed to walk into higher understanding on his own, regardless of where he is in his spiritual growth. We cannot force anyone! Even God Himself is bound and restricted by this law of free will. Step, by sometimes infinitesimal step, we raise the thinking of each person. And we *must* accept that!

If we were to love, help, and encourage from this side only

when everything was perfect on earth, we would never be able to come to your imperfect planet. This is not to say that all is hopeless, or that there are not good people everywhere. Without such people earth would be in much greater peril than she is now. But the overall level of understanding according to His ultimate will for mankind is lagging far behind His design. And the cause of this lagging is mostly found in human selfishness. Much of this theme has to do with a more recent writing in which I explained man's need to walk against the pain to overcome. Selfishness is the greatest source of this pain. We shall keep to this theme as you explore it. You need to see not only your own shortcomings but the solution(s) as well. We bring you back to causes and to solutions.

Earlier we touched in with the thought of working on yourself. You often think that failures will make us pull away our support. This is short-sighted. We are not with you just for your mediumship. We are not with you conditionally. We are with you for the long haul. Now, if you were totally to abandon all scruples and forward movement, our working together would be in jeopardy. This is true of everyone. But we are together because we are working out imperfections on all levels, inner and outer. We are here to assist you to work out your salvation, for we need salvation through our cooperative efforts. This will gather increasing clarity as time unfolds.

We *do not* see earth as you do or as the masses of humanity see. Our perspective is entirely different. Our view is from the top, from all sides, from all angles. Yours is often only a small opening through which you peer. Know the difference in perspectives. We *are* with you for the long haul.

Negative Thinking Is Your Worst Enemy

We will again and again encourage *only* positive thinking in you. We cannot, must not, deal on any other level. Negative thinking contains energies so distasteful from this side. It is distasteful from your side, too, but you cannot see as we see. We state again! These energies are dark and swirl around each soul that maintains them. As they swirl and move about, they re-enter the mind to create confusion and depression. Each time another body of negative expletives comes forth from the soul's being, whether from the mind, heart, or mouth, the darkened energies are added to like a cancerous growth and the soul is pulled down even more. How can we help such a person?

On earth you look upon cancer with such horror and fear. Negative thought in all manifestations is far more harmful to the soul: cancer and other diseases can result from this energy within man. All of this you do not see. You are more a victim of negative thinking than of any other single element in your life. So we will continue to bring you, wherever and whenever possible, into the positive, affirmative side of life. When you finally grasp this reality as your greatest and truest enemy, you will not hesitate to stop it in your life; you will run from it. Progress in human evolution is most frequently inhibited by retrograde thinking.

From this side we see each soul walking knowingly and unknowingly toward God and his own higher self. We see many diligently setting out with firm resolve and determination. But again and again we see each of you turn back in your thinking. And you have accepted this turning back as necessary and natural. It is not! It is a lie to your own being! Thoughts are energy to be managed by the intelligence of man. He can determine absolutely what thoughts will dominate his being. And each time he gives in to lesser, self-inhibiting thoughts, he reinforces his own ultimate defeat. More souls are killed by negative thinking per day than are animals and humans by guns or other destructive earthly instruments. Negative thinking is your worst enemy! Negative thinking is your worst enemy! Conversely, positive, affirmative thinking is your truest and best friend.

Become Lord of Your Thoughts

In your world you attract forces by the sum total of your being. This includes inherited potential and merit as well as to some extent inherited spiritual problems. This inheritance varies so with each individual that we are hard pressed to categorize specifically. Wide problem areas might be placed in broad divisions. We see the innate and inherited potential. All of this goes into each soul's makeup.

We want to emphasize here the role that thought energy—cumulative and spontaneous and momentary—has in determining what forces are drawn to you. If you fluctuate between extremes of thought you will draw forces from both sides of the scale—negative to positive. They will do battle over you to form tighter bonds, one to pull you down and one to pull you up. Some spirits are drawn to sheer energy, not truly aware of what they do. Still others are positive but over-excited, and go beyond the boundary of common sense positivity, causing their counterparts on earth to suffer these extremes. This creates a treadmill of extreme ups and downs. And of course there are all shades of darkness and light between these two extremes.

It is not easy, therefore, to break these bonds, especially when the masses accept such behavior as a part of *normal* human reality. Going to extremes is not man's original intended nature. As long as man accepts such behavior as normal—and we underline "accept," because there is freedom of choice—he will remain a victim of his own thoughts.

It is true that habits deeply embedded in the human psyche become solidified in time into impenetrable forms. But the beginning of freedom is man's proclaiming to all negativity within himself and others that he is lord of his thoughts and he shall command his mind to rise and walk toward the light. And while so doing he will march against the foes of negative thoughts, which, because he gave them life and breath, will actively work to sabotage and stop him, and pull him down into the swirling darkness of despair and depression.

Behind every flank of marching, resistant, negative thoughts is a spiritual force that will enter in as it has a thousand times before, seeking to stop the poor soul from rising. What we speak of here is not a fairy tale conjured up from undisciplined imagination. We cry out a truth, a reality, that we see and shrink from on earth. It is our single greatest sorrow to observe from this side!

Only You Can Win Your Own Freedom

We return to you as our charge and fellow worker in this desperate need to march forward and upward. You must steel yourself to stand by your ongoing conviction to proclaim and obtain freedom from negativity in every form! Regardless of what others may do or say you must seek your freedom now! You must reverse your inhibited thought that you can never rise or never change!

Do for and unto others out of sincere caring, and know that if the base of such action is love it will return to you and bless you. *Nothing* that we do is outside the law of returning kind. Love when it hurts to love. Move against the desire or temptation to withhold love. You and you alone can win your freedom!

Your writings at this stage are not for yourself alone. We speak to all within the reading audience of these words. We are desperate to bring this good news to earth. Your contemporary philosophers and writers are but a wave washing upon the earth today touched by the truth of which we speak—the power of positive thinking. But even most of them do not know the true and ultimate power of positive thinking. Even they are shackled by lesser, inhibiting thoughts. They too must perceive more.

Jesus' Message Revolutionized Man's Thinking

The good news of Jesus 2000 years ago contained the proclamation of positive thoughts, thoughts totally centered upon his Father's business, resulting in the Kingdom of God upon earth in man. To accept Jesus and all that he came for, the people of the day needed new minds. Most could not, would not, think as he thought. Reformation on a full scale, 100 percent attendance to the higher calling, could not begin.

Rather, thoughts filled with power-seeking, selfishness, and impurity of all kinds blocked Jesus' way to higher thoughts within his contemporaries. Only by returning again and again to the source of all power-generating thoughts could Jesus replenish himself and go on. Jesus came to start a revolution in the *thinking* of man! That revolution is still going on; bringing God's kingdom on earth remains our divine mandate! We are part of that wave, that revolution. We pray that for your sake you will hear the need within yourself as you read our words to change the direction and content of your thinking so that His kingdom in all its love and light can dawn fully within you. Remember, only you can do it for you!

Because of the tendency on the part of many to set firm their mental jaw with determination to live positively, we speak more.

We know from this side that many latter-day philosophies have covered the earth, philosophies which massage man into good feelings and efforts toward positive thinking. Some of them, though couched in beautiful language and bound in beautiful covers, do not say that much. A number of them have helped considerably in causing their readers to examine more fully the influence of thought upon life's unfolding circumstances. This is so good. But we want to move you to action, dear reader! You must establish a practical approach to changing the negative record of thought you play within your mind day after day. Unless a philosophy be livable what use is it? So lest we sound like spiritually empty poets and philosophers, we want to offer some practical solutions.

Acknowledge and Claim Your Own Goodness

First, you must see your goodness and your potential. And in doing so, you must affirm both. While it is true that He who made us is far above us upon the scale of love, we must not wrongfully compare and thereby nullify the value He placed within us.

There is a difference between laying claim to having caused goodness within ourselves and giving God credit for whatever goodness we see. Jesus said, "No one is good but God." By this he meant only God is absolutely all love, all good. Man contains elements of intrinsic goodness resultant from God's goodness in man, but man also contains elements of evil. In this sense, truly only God has been good.

To downgrade yourself constantly while trying at the same time to be positive works confusion and havoc within the human psyche. There are those caught in this paradox who simply do not grow, because while on one hand they affirm, they at the same time deny. It is a new time, a new age. The old concepts belong to a lesser day. God today wants and needs man to proclaim his sonship. It is a matter of emphasis. If I think my goodness derives from self-creation without the handiwork of God, I err. But to acknowledge my goodness as derived from Him is to glorify Him correctly. So for His sake we must proclaim and nurture this goodness within.

Displace Negativity with Realistic Positivity

Secondly, we urge you not to waste energy upon denial. Admit what is wrong with you. See your negative thinking for what it is. You cannot leave your enemy behind unless you see and know him. Still, you cannot be a Pollyanna and believe that if you simply ignore it, negative thinking will go away. See it objectively. Do not enter into battle with it or engage in self-castigation. If you do, you are caught back into its web. Rather, see your negative thinking and know the details of its appearance. Each time negativity tries to capture your attention you can recognize the tell-tale signs and can turn away, putting distance between you and "it." Be ready then to protect yourself and raise yourself by affirming your goodness. Make *affirmations* your fellow soldiers in the battle to rise. Let them protect you and lift you. And know that as you do so, you will become stronger and stronger. It is a displacement, replacement process. As you fill your mind with positivity, realistic positivity, you displace negativity. By ignoring its efforts to pull you back and down you cease to give it power over your life. By spending even a moment's notice you re-engage it. In the engaging/resisting process you enter again into the age-old battle for freedom of thought.

Thought Is Energy, Thought Is Real, Thought Has Power

Thirdly, you must acknowledge the reality of energy though it is yet invisible in some forms to your sight on earth. Energy is real. You are energy. Thought is energy, and energy in any form when set in motion moves ever forward, seeking an object with which to unite to fulfill its intrinsic role, design, and structure. Elements within the form automatically dictate its course and its influence.

Negative thought is energy set in a particular molecular form, containing a particular life, set forth upon a course. It is a living entity created by man, not having individualized, God-given character, but, nevertheless, a character given by man. Enough negative thoughts gathered together coupled with accompanying spiritual forces can and do weaken and destroy.

Thoughts, whatever their content, are not abstract. They are real and have life as animated by and through man. In accord with inner content, man's thoughts go in advance of his earthly life, paving the road to come, and drawing to him that which he thinks about day after day. This is a cosmic fact. Man does to a large, large extent create his own reality and *does* indeed experience self-fulfilling prophecies.

Had man not left the Lord of lofty and loving thoughts, man's thoughts would have paved a road toward heaven on earth and would have drawn to himself only goodness. But now his ignorance contaminates his path, blocks his way, and draws to himself energies unworthy of his original divinely attuned being.

The Proper Use of Energy Guarantees Success

Meditate long upon our words. You will find power in them: God designed the world for *success* through the proper use of energy. He sent forth His thought into the vacuum waiting to be filled. He meditated for eons upon the future and paved the way to the eventual cosmos with thoughts only of success and love. He then drew to Himself, out of Himself, beings called angels that could help Him fulfill this dream.

He still thinks and dreams so. And whoever dreams with Him will find transformation and true power! We bless these words to the heart of the reader.

In His holy name and to the proclamation of His holy thought we stand by ever ready to help you and Him in this upward evolution to peace on earth, in heaven, and in His heart.

Saint Germain and All!

6:00 A.M.
April 29, 1988
Burke, Virginia

You need not stretch your imagination to know I am here and in place. Soon, very soon, everything will become clearer. I will be closer, and contact you more directly. We need to touch in briefly just to keep the relationship flowing. You are being tested these days and while you may waver you will and are passing through these times successfully. Grasp the essentials as you are inspired and stick with them. We will be very, very close this week as you plan and execute.

Dwell Only on Positive Solutions

We want to remind you to dwell not on the negative but upon positive solutions. Come to know what negative is in subtle form. Remember, that which is counter to His laws is classified as negative. Certain fundamental attitudes may not appear evil, but in their unfolding are affecting your life course and are very destructive.

We used the word "evil" because all negativity that is counter to His spiritual principles is destructive to the human soul. It is this negativity in subtle form that is most insidious and undermining. Words like "I can't," or "this is impossible," or many other daily habits of negation against potential are inhibiting forms of energy and keep you from realizing your perfection.

Immerse Yourself in His Presence

We would emphasize staying close to and remaining one with His word. Pray much and meditate daily. Better to immerse yourself in His presence and let Him guide and purify you by His closeness. As you turn again and again to Him these days, the constructive, the positive, the holy will manifest in you. We must allow Him to take over and supplant our inner chambers of thought and feeling. And He will!

Man's biggest obstacle to overcoming is not evil itself, but rather man's not turning continually to Him. To enter in and fight evil by constant opposition is not the way, as we have instructed you before. Rather, spend your energies to find the ways and means of drawing closer and closer to Him, and stay with Him. This is the source of all right, positive, and prosperous living.

While we have repeated ourselves here somewhat, it is necessary to remind you of your right course of action: He *within* us is greater than the world without. The secret then is to open the heart to allow Him entrance, and to keep it open so that He can remain within.

Here is man's area of endeavor, here is where you now must work more and more. Do as we instruct, and you will rise; you will triumph. Don't allow *anyone* to deter you from your practices. Take them with you!

We are very, very close and shall remain so.

All of our support and love,
Saint Germain and All

8:26 A.M.
May 15, 1988
Burke, Virginia

CHAPTER THIRTEEN

THE PRINCIPLE OF REPETITION AND THE ART OF SUCCESS

We wanted most to impress you today with "going with the tide." You have surfed. You have stood watching the waves appear in the distance out in the ocean's waters. As each one moved toward you, you judged whether it was the one to ride to the shore. Some you judged too small, and you let them pass. Then—perhaps after several waves—you saw one coming and prepared yourself to catch it and ride it in. This timing, this catching the right wave, is all important and an art within the art of surfing. We want you to keep this imagery in mind, drawing upon it today and in the coming days.

Thoughts Are the Pictures in Our Mind

We are talking first of attitude. Think only success. Do not think limitation. We have told you that your thoughts are sent forth in time, preceding your physical arrival. These thoughts pave the way and determine your path. If you constantly send forth thoughts of doubt or worry or suspicion, or thoughts of negativity of any kind, you will meet them along the way as they return to you in your external and internal environment.

As you think so you become. Your thoughts—positive, negative, or a combination—directly determine the level and quality of your overall life energies. Therefore, the quality of your thoughts is all-important in determining the *outcome* of your spiritual and physical life. Self-mastery *begins* with mastery of thought.

Thinking is a word used to describe the *activity* of the mind. Thinking produces thoughts, which come in many forms, sizes, and shapes. All that exists in creation was at one time a thought in God's mind.

However simple or complex the manifestation of thoughts, the mind seeks to make meaning out of them by turning them into pictures. This is so in your world and in ours. These thought pictures influence the production of other related thought pictures. These can, if taken to the nth degree, create a sizable network of interrelated thoughts. Pictures in the mind, whether constructive or destructive, exert much influence upon the will, as like slides or movies they play over and over in the mind. Out of this reality of mind activity comes the willpower to act upon our thoughts.

Thought and its influence upon outcome is so serious that in order to create a life of success spiritually and physically, we must be ever alert regarding the quality of our thoughts so as to eliminate any and all destructive thoughts and to foster only constructive ones.

Align Your Thoughts with Life's Highest Values

We say to all, you must change your attitude, the direction of your thoughts, 180 degrees toward love, goodness, truth, and beauty if you truly want to prosper in life. As you work to change your thoughts, the pictures, as a part of the overall thoughts, will change. Sometimes as you change the pictures 180 degrees or whatever degree is necessary, new thoughts and tributaries of thoughts are formed.

You speak on earth of "changing life-styles." It is a popular thought today. What does it mean practically? Many try to change the location and content of their daily life. They change their style of clothing, food, and living surroundings—all to meet the pictures they have in mind for what is meaningful. Society has been changed in your world by the constant input of advertising. Human values have been affected by this constant pictorial, verbal input into the minds of the masses. This has been planned influence. American society especially has been carefully ushered into its present state, manipulated by a relatively small group of people. It is not change by conscious association alone, but is change created by affecting people's desires subconsciously, making them think that they want or need some particular thing.

Not all of these changes have been bad; many are good. We want you to note however, that fads in America, or the world for that matter, come in waves through massive, intensive advertising. Even the need factor is instilled, in which case many people *have* to have something: a calculator, a new style of curling iron, the latest elaborate toaster, and so on. They acquire them only to find that they didn't really need them at all. The need factor was simply part of the hype. All modern psychology addresses human conditioning, which works because it is how we are influenced, how we are molded, how we "image" and line out these images and on and on.

Constant Attendance to Spiritual Practice Is Vital

We bring this to your attention to see and study clearly how thoughts, ideas, and pictures are so potent when repeated and repeated. Most of humanity today is out of control. They have little or no awareness of the power of their thoughts in creating their own future reality and, collectively, the reality of the world. Pavlov's dog is a milestone historical mark in the mind of modern man. Here, by experimentation and observation, man realized a great and central truth about being and existence: "Man can be changed by repetition." And when his *emotions* are significantly affected he is more deeply, easily, rapidly changed. This is a universal truth and in itself is good! In the hands of self-centered men, however, it has been dangerously applied, cruelly applied, and has caused untold suffering.

We want to say this: Man's return to God is experienced by the use of this same universal principle. When we pray repeatedly and visualize consciously or unconsciously that which we pray for, it will come to pass. When a man, woman, or child is immersed in the environment of love centered on God and His ultimate will, he or she is transformed. But to achieve this spiritual state, and through it higher elevation, there must be a constant attendance to spiritual practice. Because man is prone to new ideas and quick fixes he can easily deviate from the spiritual path. This process we speak of must contain not only repetition, but also vividly portrayed images of man-in-God. It must have an underlying emotional appeal to allow these images and the whole process to sink deep within the soul. Not only must the thoughts and the pictures be changed, but also the heart. And when man is freely involved in this transformational process he is accompanied by those in spirit, including Almighty God Himself, who reinforce and make more and more real what the path-walker has been seeking in practice, in mental imagery, and in his heart-feeling.

We draw your attention to this analogy. When you prepare to visit someone at a distance, you visualize that person and his surroundings. If it is a trip for a reunion, you experience flashes of that person in your mind. You also reflect and recall former times in emotional and pictorial form. This kindles within you an even more ardent desire to see the person, to get there more quickly. To your practical sense, this is only mind-stuff and not reality.

To the inventor the process is the same. He sees within his mind's eye an invention. His being becomes totally involved in creating it. In both cases—the one on his way to a reunion and the inventor—the inner workings, the inner dynamics, are the same and carry the individual along the way until he or she arrives at the reality. Our journey back to our true self and to God is no different. Just as the repetition of thought about seeing a loved one carried us along the mental, emotional, physical path to the actual reality, so our daily life-path toward God influences us in the same way. The closer we get to the reality of what we have imagined and hoped for, the easier it is for Him to magnify and substantiate that reality until one day we stand in His waiting arms and all good and true visions become a living tableau with Him.

False Sentiment Hinders Soul Progression

So powerful are man's mental/spiritual creative faculties, a gift from God, that he may falsely believe heaven to consist of certain erroneous manifestations. He solidifies these false ideas so concretely within his mind while on earth—through repetition, prayer, and emotions—that when he arrives in spirit world, the ideas of his mind, the pictures of his mind, the emotions of his heart exist as living, solidified energy, reflecting the sum total of his ideas while on earth. We cannot say enough about the power of thought and the consequences of right and wrong thinking!

Many in religious circles on earth speak of their belief in sentimental sentences. Sentiment, true sentiment, has its place. But it has little or nothing to do with objective, spiritual living. We would not wish that anyone be devoid of feelings, but they must be appropriate feelings. Many hold to outworn concepts because of the emotional attachment derived from sentiments. Some keep the belongings of deceased loved ones. This is fine to a point. But if done to an extreme, it is foolish and misplaced sentiment. Extreme sentiment creates energies that draw a departed soul back and down to the earth plane, hindering his advancement. This is misapplied, inappropriate sentiment that may seek to keep a memory alive, but by being erroneously fixed in the past actually hinders soul progression.

Humility in and of itself means little. Humility is a vibratory state of mind and heart through which, by greater passivity and openness, God can more easily enter in to help us and be with us. Yet many, out of emotional attachment, have made a religion of piety. Those who still wear the outmoded religious trappings of yesteryear but do not embody true spirituality are living in pure sentiment. It is laughable from this side to see so much devotion to form devoid of true inner understanding or spirituality. It is well and good to use clothing and environment to help create certain desirable inner spiritual qualities. But, take care not to feel justified by appearances alone while your soul starves for true spiritual sustenance.

Go Over, Around, or Under All Obstacles

Take the wave now! The timing is right. All is in place. All the right conditions are in place. But the most important conditions are within you. So watch carefully. Now is not the time to harbor thoughts of self-doubt, fear, or insecurity. Go with that to which you have been aspiring. Realize that where you are and what you are is the result of the sum total of all the energies you have been generating. It could not be otherwise. And while you have been tempted to quit or alter circumstances, such thought is just that— temptation. It is very clear that all the timing says "go for it" in every area of your life! Know that this is resultant and also that you are closer and closer to the reality of the things you have up to now only prayed for, dreamed about, and longed for!!! Were we able to shout in your ear with all the force at our command, we would! Do not be misled by illusions or by others' ideas or concepts. You have seen the wisdom and value of all that you are about. Stick with it and resist all retrograde thoughts or actions. Avoid all obstacles in your way. Go over, under, or around them.

Rework and solidify your plan; then execute it. Work patiently and systematically. Do not for a moment look back or dwell upon despair or limitations. Only time stands between us and our ideals. Limitation is an illusion, for if we endure and hold fast to our ideals, we will realize them.

Advance by regrouping your ideas. As we have taught you, execute everything systematically. As you pass beyond this time, your merit will be such that things will become easier and major obstacles will begin to disappear.

As for prophecies, some can be changed—most can be changed. If you desire to speed up or alter an aspect, that too is within your own capacity. Decide to be successful and apply yourself. Sometimes we are foiled by images that contain success but within a certain scope or time period. You can destroy or prolong things by impetuosity. However, you can positively transform things too, if you are willing to pay the correct price. At least you have to try. The most important thing is always to do things in harmony with universal law.

Thoughts Affect Your Spiritual Energy Pattern

We wanted to address how energy changes around us. You have been experiencing greater and greater awareness of your own sensitivity. This is vital as it is this aspect of who you are that is so important and useful to your life's work. We do not want to change this; we in fact are working on your energies to direct and heighten this sensitivity. You are not a robot or radar that we use like some common piece of equipment. Rather, while we work with your energies, we seek mutual cooperation. Repeatedly, we discourse about your sensitivity and the role of your consciousness in protecting and directing it. We are working on the energies of your being in the mental, emotional, and physical realms. We do this, as part of helping man on earth, with everyone. However, with one destined to your kind of work we are able to work more closely toward attunement. But, we again emphasize your humanness and free will, lest we sound like auto mechanics.

Recently, last night as a matter of fact, we tried to impress you with exactly what happens under certain circumstances that bring you down.

Man's Extremity Is God's Opportunity

First, you must be most acutely aware that the atomic, and thus the molecular configuration in your mind (your spirit energy pattern) is changed with the intrusion of lesser thoughts. This is not choice or chance; it is absolute. It can indeed be called a science. The overall spiritual atmosphere then in turn affects your physical vibration, stimulating physical responses within the body. These energies of your being *are real*. The control switch or button is thought. If you begin to turn the switch to lesser, negative, selfish thoughts, the energies will go down and you will be affected. The dimmer in your dining room serves in the same way thoughts serve in your total being.

Whether it is the horse before the cart, or vice-versa, you are passing through this way of experience through which you can teach others. This is the up side of your experience. The down side is that you suffer and prolong your suffering as you pass through these experiences. We do not want justification to reign here. Nor do we say it is necessary or okay to direct activity to anything lesser than God and His will.

In accordance with the laws of spiritual growth, we want to turn your energies to constructive ends and give meaning to your suffering. This is God's way. Metaphorically speaking, "what the devil causes, God takes and uses to raise man." "Man's extremity is God's opportunity." He has no other choice, for He must work within man and must find ways to convert lesser energies to serve His higher purposes. Teaching you by first allowing you to suffer until you stand back and see it for what it is, and then leading you to see deeper aspects of cause and effect, and finally inspiring you to remove yourself from error, is His overall instruction to us. This is the patient love of a Father working out the salvation of His children. Love knows no other way.

You are beginning to see, and in seeing, you are beginning to substantially change your thinking and your inner slide show. Be patient and work carefully to acquire the new self. It is coming. Re-read our words to you and never doubt either our love or our leadership. We are with you for the full course. Know that we suffer with you. But we hold only unconditional love as our banner flying high before our united vanguard for Him!

Saint Germain with Brother Joseph

10:42 A.M.
May 12, 1988
West Grove, Pennsylvania

CHAPTER FOURTEEN

MEDITATION: MAN'S JOURNEY TO FIND GOD WITHIN

Each must stand alone, knowing that God dwells in him. Each must respect himself as an instrument of God. Without God within there is no life without. You cannot separate the word LIFE from the word GOD. There is no life without Him.

God Is the Cause and Core of All Life

These words are simple but so profound in practice. God, the core of all life, sends forth, from his mind and heart, individualized rays of energy—in the form of white light—into each of His children where He manifests as the everlasting Spirit within the spirit of man.

God is the cause and core of your individualized existence. This is why when you can see from an elevated level you can see all things are truly one.

It is God as the core of life that is the uniting energy making all things one. There can never be any complete separation from this energy. If that were possible you would not need God and could be a god unto yourself. Though man has fallen away from God, God is still present as the life within the soul.

Can a parent's heart ever forget his offspring? No, and neither can God. Had God been able to be completely separate from man

He could have let man go. But history does not show us that He has left us alone. Rather, we see evidence of greater and greater influence by God through the evolution of man's mind to greater and greater compassion, sensitivity to his fellow man, equality between the sexes, and so on. Man is gravitating increasingly toward unity at the center of life and in the outer reaches of life.

This is the influence of God. This work, this movement toward unity under the banner of world brotherhood in truth and love, is God's work. It will not be stopped!

God's Divinity Dwells within You

We stand again and again to remind you all of your role in this evolution of mankind. But you must realize God is within you now! There is separation, and therefore distance, between your consciousness and God's presence only because of ignorance. God, the Father is *already* present in you. He stands as light within the center of your mind and your heart. He speaks to you with parental guidance constantly. You were created so that He can dwell fully within you and shine out through the portals of your character and personality.

Is this so hard to comprehend? Does an apple tree not contain the original energy of the seed from which it came? Was not the seed's original energy the source of life within the tiny emerging tree that later became fully grown? And could you take that "seed" energy from the tree and still have "life" within the tree?

The answer is simply and obviously "No!" My brothers and sisters, children of our Father in heaven, are you not greater than this tree which grows fruit? Yes! You are! Then is not God's energy in you? Yes! It is! But you are more than a tree or rock, or a bird of the air, or a fish of the water. If they all contain the life of life, do you not contain this life and more?

Trees and rocks, birds and fish, cannot love and reason as humans. So there is something more of Him in us through which to express Himself. It is not the energy itself that makes mankind uniquely divine. Since His energy exists in every form on earth and in spirit, He is everywhere and everything is divine. But man is divine in the highest meaning of the word because that part of God that literally dwells within man is His love and His intelligence through which He communicates with man and through which man can discern love and truth and thereby all phenomena of the cosmos.

I am so thrilled, so utterly ecstatic to speak of Him in this way, for I know from experience that this is so. And to speak so is to experience an even deeper, greater portion of Him within myself. It makes me long to help others discover this simple but magnificently profound reality within themselves.

True Morality Is Divine Human Conduct

If a man truly sees and knows that he sees God within a fellow human being, can he in any way harm, abuse, or mistreat that person? Would he, upon seeing this light within, want to have It hurt within himself? No! No! No! He would not!

We must push aside as quickly as possible the lesser issues of life and the world situation and bring mankind to this inner awareness! Ultimately, the world cannot be changed from darkness into light until man has this inner revelation of God's existence within himself and his brothers and sisters. From this realization and inner experience of Him come those true, unchanging standards of human conduct we all call morality. Hearing words of morality is lesser than seeing God within the human soul through the gift of spiritual sight. The first is theory, the latter is reality.

When we surrender to God, we lose nothing. Instead, we discard unnecessary coverings of pride and other forms of corruption to discover He was there all the time waiting to emerge and lead us to heaven. To surrender is to lose nothing that is truly, eternally important. No! When we surrender we find the meaning of eternity in love. We discover the true self, the center of which is God—alive and dwelling always and forever in man.

Meditation: the Great Journey Inward

Today meditation is so greatly emphasized on earth. The reason is because that journey inward is the last one man will make to discover the cause and purpose of life. This inner journey is necessary and is inspired by God. He is calling out loudly and clearly from within the hearts of all mankind, even those whose lack of awareness dims the shining light within. But in time they too will be reached.

If you are yearning to find the purpose of life and the cause of suffering, and if He truly dwells there on earth in the core of the souls of mankind, how much He wants to be heard and emerge into the total awareness of man. If you search, pulled beyond your control, to find answers, then it is He calling within your own being to do so.

The prodigal son is your fallen self longing now to come home. The Father waiting to meet you has never left the homestead, but rather has been calling out to you from the center of your own being to come home:

> Come inward to the light! Hear Me already inside of your heart, the home of your being; I am already present and waiting. Search no further. I am here! I am so close you cannot see Me. Step back from your state of mind and emotions which

often block your view of Me and then you will see Me!

And when you do see and experience Me with all your faculties of discernment, don't be surprised if you cry in joy and sorrow. Joy because you have at last found the King within the kingdom of your heart and sorrow because you have missed Me more than human words can say and because you are sorry you didn't know I was here all the time.

I have spoken to you with all the power at My command. In seasons of sorrow I have cried with you. And sometimes as you thought you spoke to yourself, after the cleansing, you were speaking to Me.

At other times when you experienced unspeakable joy you spoke to Me thanking Me. I heard. I was moved, and leapt within your heart and echoed your joys.

In all of this between the sorrows and the joys I have never left you. I have always been here. And I shall never leave you. There is a beautiful land here within your Soul of souls. I stay here because love will not let Me leave. I am a happy prisoner of love. I wanted it this way and love compelled Me to create you so.

I shall stay here no matter how long it takes to bring you through the gates of your true self. And if I suffer, and I do suffer to stay here, it is all worth it. I dream again and again of your return and this sustains My heart to stay and stay. I wait with untiring love to see you come home. Don't be long in returning for it will ease your sorrow and Mine to hold you within My eternal, abiding love.

I conclude today, having brought the Father's words and heart to earth through this message. He is the poet of poets, the lover of lovers. He is true and He lives within each of us. Let us be on the way, beloved ones, in the journey inward to Him.

Know His love ever stays with you. We come with that love shining brightly to beckon the way onto the path back home.

Saint Germain

6:20 A.M.
May 29, 1988
West Grove, Pennsylvania

CHAPTER FIFTEEN

OVERCOMING LIMITATIONS BY MASTERING YOUR THOUGHTS

There are no limitations. The limitations that confront you are made manifest from your perspective alone. You have set ideas that limit you. In reality you are a free agent and can do as you wish.

Within God's Principles There Are No Limitations

When we speak of no limitations we *mean no* limitations. Of course, you want to limit yourself in the incorrect use of your life's energies. Evil exists because man *is* free and has misused his energies. So it goes without saying that when we speak of limitations we mean that you do not limit yourself within the scope of God's principles. All things that are good are possible within His principles.

Let your energies flow today and this week. It is important that you seek self-direction and self-control more than anything. You have realized today, upon awakening, that life is not all orderly, that there remain many loose ends. But we want to emphasize that in order to meet the challenge of overcoming you must focus not upon outward circumstances but within yourself. Do not think, "How can I overcome, accomplish, or complete something?" Rather, look into yourself and seek within your own being for the answer to questions of success. In order to find success you have to find self-control, self-discipline. Everything we accomplish in life is wrought by directing mental, emotional, and physical energies toward specific goals.

Gain Outer Control by Mastering Inner Control

As you write you will not reach conclusions or have a feeling of satisfaction unless you follow through and come to conclusions by which you can make decisions and take action. Too often you look at your day and see what faces you to be done. Frequently you feel overwhelmed. This is because you see your responsibilities as dominating you. It is the other way around. You are to be master over your responsibilities. By way of self-mastery you come to master your daily duties. When you are overwhelmed by what faces you it is because you are not in control of your *inner* existence. Things seem impossible to manage because you are not in charge of managing yourself. This is self-mastery—to work within, to determine precisely what thoughts and feelings shall predominate. Better yet, "How shall I think and feel about my daily duties?"

Within the realm of God's principles we must choose constructive, positive thoughts, positive solutions and ideas with which to approach our daily duties. Our point is: Do not continue your pre-programmed response to that which faces you daily. Choose new ways of thinking. Give yourself a chance and do not demand perfection. We must come to understand the rhythm of life. A heart that does not keep its steady, pre-set rhythm can work havoc upon the mind, emotions, and actions of a person. Life must ebb and flow. There are central things and there are peripheral things in life. The central things are first, and their completion leads to things more external and peripheral. When we allow ourselves to lose perspective and thereby take untimely actions we throw off our whole tempo. Most people are not in control; have not been in control most of their lives. Why? Because they are not aware of their need to be in control in the way outlined above. Humanity must be taught how to think correctly.

Focus on Eternal Values

Most of a life's accomplishments are forgotten as the life unfolds toward its earthly departure. More and more as we approach life's transition, we look inward to what we have *become*. It is this way because what we have become is that which we will see upon our arrival into the finer eternal vibrations. Our earthly life experiences (we begin to recognize) were but circumstances to allow us to see ourselves, to direct ourselves, to master ourselves. The sooner we realize this great spiritual truth the sooner we can live correctly, the sooner we can find and maintain the God-given tempo of our being. It is another one of these do-it-now instructions.

We began today by speaking of limitations. And if our thinking is not clear and principled we work against the purposes of God. Today God does not so much care about your external activities. In fact, the only things you *must* do is seek Him first and attend to your personal relationship with Him and His spiritual laws. Then all things shall follow in correct, rhythmic order. This is central and all other things are secondary. To attend Him is not to go off somewhere and do ritual for a certain number of minutes or hours. To attend is to speak with Him, to consult, to seek through His presence within you and through His objective principles around you, to know, understand, and do His will. And do not be misled into believing that only physical action will suffice. Sometimes physical *inactivity*, with passive meditation or thinking in order to reflect and understand is the necessity of the day. To run headlong into the day may not be the best way to accomplish your life's intended goals.

So, do not limit yourself with out-moded, inappropriate thinking. Realize clearly how you have allowed yourself to be overwhelmed by life's circumstances because you were not in control of the instrument panel of your mind and emotions. To start the day, as you have today, is to push the "first button" first in the sequence of buttons to be pushed throughout the day. Remember this and seek to practice it. And do not continue to be overwhelmed.

Inner Reflection Is Crucial

Some will read our words and speak disparagingly of them because they insist they have no time for reflection, to think upon these weightier things of life. They "simply have no time!" "Then," we ask, "when will they have time for their inner life?" Aren't these people out of control? Isn't life running them? When will they have time to take care of and cultivate an inner world of unity and peace with their Creator?

It is recognized, of course, that God is in action too, not just in the reflective, contemplative state, especially is this so in today's fast paced world. We do not deny this.

What we say to the one who denies himself time for going inward concerns necessity and limited thinking. You *need* an inner life now! Otherwise, you are avoiding the real you and your real, eternal needs and eternal realities. Unless you reflect you will never realize the eternal "you" deep inside who needs to be fed with correct thinking and feeling, through which alone you achieve correct actions. To reflect as recommended—to go inside and search around with the light of honesty—may require adjustments in thinking as well as in our outer life activities. But we say that unless you do all of this for yourself you may never achieve what you were born to achieve on this earth—to fulfill the actual purpose of your earthly walk. All of life's circumstances on earth are placed there for man to overcome by mastering self. Man is not to be mastered by the events in the unfolding of life. We must understand all of this even to begin to reflect, prioritize, or act correctly! We must demand of ourselves new thinking modes, new ways of looking at life. When we are unhappy we must look inside to see if we are unhappy because there is no way out or because of the way that we look at life. Usually, almost always, it is the latter and not the former.

Be True to Your Eternal Goals

In conclusion, as you approach the day first go within and get things straight at the beginning point of actions. Secondly, make sure you prioritize your unfolding day. Cut out what is superficial and unnecessary—regardless of what others may say or think. Be true to yourself and your *eternal* goals! Thirdly, look at your list of life's tasks and be master over them. If they are practical musts in order to maintain earthly, physical life, see them so, knowing they must be done in order to exist, to fulfill earthly duties. But do not see these responsibilities merely as a list of "things to do." Rather, see that in order to do them you must work with your energies—mental, emotional, and physical—objectively. You must become a spiritual master by choosing to do these things through conscious volition: "I am taking responsibility for my outer life by determining what attitude and thoughts shall guide my inner life. Through each of these steps of reflection before action I am mastering myself!"

Reflect day by day upon this philosophy and you will begin very soon to see a new person emerge. We will not describe this new person for we want you to discover this newly emerging self on your own. Do not continue to limit yourself but go inward and break up the limitations by seeing life through an eternal perspective and discard—through this reflective, inner action— old, outmoded, inappropriate thoughts. Build an eternal you that is mastered and whole.

We close with love and support always,
Saint Germain and Band

6:35 A.M.
May 31, 1988
West Grove, Pennsylvania

Part Four
Transformation of Self

CHAPTER SIXTEEN

TRANSFORMATION THROUGH PRAYER AND ACTION

The key words today are: It is not what you *pray* for that you get; rather, your internal spiritual state determines what you shall draw to yourself. You must be and act in accordance with your prayers at all times. In this way you *become* what you pray for and draw to yourself the answers to your prayers according to your becoming.

You Draw to Yourself What You Are

Everything in the cosmos is vibratory, in both your world and ours. Vibrations must be harmonious to exist side by side or together. How then can you draw to yourself anything different from what you are internally? It is impossible. As all things operate by universal, cosmic principles, there can be no faking, no pretense, no sham. It is our message today to say loudly and clearly: You draw to yourself exactly what you are. If you cry and cry to the heavens but find your prayers unanswered, you must ask yourself the condition of your own heart. "Ye are gods" means the power of creativity and re-creativity of self belongs to you and is in your hands. To become this *real* self—not the self you pretend to be or parade as an actor to the world, but the *real* self—you must be 100 percent honest with yourself. To do this we stand to aid you in the confrontation, stage by stage, in dealing with the pains of seeing yourself as you truly are. But unless you go through this process of seeing your true inner self and overcoming you cannot be transformed. It is not enough to spend time and call it progress. The walk of spiritual faith is not a mere passage of time from one point to another, but rightfully consists of growth through transformation.

Little by little as you truly face yourself with courage and don't flinch or pull back and work systematically upon yourself, under the guidance, love, and protection of spirit, your vibration changes, and in this gradual transformation process, you draw to yourself higher and higher levels of success, accomplishments, and rewards.

God Is The Light in Your Soul

We have said it before and will say it again: your life upward is the process of uncovering God's presence within you, hidden beneath self and "sin." As your higher self—your self as God originally idealized you—is uncovered and comes to the fore and basks more and more in the light of His presence, it grows in spiritual height and strength. It is equipped to take full leadership, potentially, as your lesser self is diminished and eventually disappears. Do not look out there somewhere, look deep inside. It is inside that you must work to release your true self and within that true self, the God-self.

Simply speaking: You are all light within and the brightness of that light depends upon the percentage that He is able to shine out fully within you. As you grow, He shines ever brighter and brighter out of the spiritual portals of your spirit. He is the light within your soul, the light within your light. You must tune in to the spiritual space within and discover these things yourself. It is your own journey inward that you must make alone. No one else can do this walk for you.

The word "good" comes from the word "God." The degree to which you are developed spiritually so that HE animates your thoughts, feelings and actions is the degree to which He is manifest in you. And this can also be said to be your goodness. The criterion for goodness is absolute, not relative. It is not one based upon national culture or social mores or so-called norms. The absolute standard is God Himself. His standard of love determines our degree of goodness. To love as He in kind, and to the fullest degree of our capacity, is to be Christ-like.

Because Jesus exemplified this love he could say: "He who has seen me has seen the Father. I am in the Father and He is in me." He came to illuminate all souls within, to turn on the light of love and truth within the hearts and minds of mankind. He stated the Kingdom was within because it is in man that God dwells most fully. And it is from the Father within that man deviated—from His standard of love to a standard of selfish love, not based upon the intrinsic beauty within man, but upon externals. As the hearts and minds of men and women became clouded, they lost their ability any longer to hear His voice or see His presence as manifested in their own beings. God became trapped and lost within deviated man—man who had deviated from the godly standard of love.

Our Journey to Heaven Is to Go Within

To comprehend the reality of which we speak is not easy for those whose hearts are far away from goodness, God's goodness. Nor is it easy to comprehend for those who believe God to be a force in some far-off place whom they must reach in spatial time. As such people reach outwardly, they do discover Him to a greater and greater degree. But ultimately they must turn within for the final miles of their journey to heaven. Heaven is not so much a place as a state of heart and mind. All that dwells there is a reflection of this inner state. To love as God loves is to feel as He feels, to think as He thinks, and to act as He acts. When you have fulfilled this commandment, you shall be at peace and filled with freedom within and with His joy. This state is heaven to the heart compared to the world's offerings, and it cannot be bought, indeed, with all the gold in the world!

Take Responsibility for Your Spiritual Growth

Many are praying and waiting for God to reach down and transform them. Often good feelings become a substitute for a true, full, and mature life in Him. Feelings are often misleading, whereas truth clarifies and tells us which path to walk, regardless of how we feel! But just how can we go about transforming ourselves? What is our portion of responsibility? It is this: "God helps those who help themselves; pray as if everything depended on God, but act as if everything depended upon you! God feeds the birds but He does not throw it in their nest."

What do these aphorisms say about man's experience in walking with and toward God? And what do they tell us about man's portion of responsibility? While He through His creative, re-creative process helps us, He cannot and will not perform our portion of responsibility. Wait as we will, we will die before we see Him take over completely and treat us as puppets or helpless children! He wants us to be adults, mature and responsible. Therefore, He must allow us to grow on our own as He influences us according to His portion of responsibility.

When we are babes, we must have complete care and attendance. We are helpless. We reach a time in our growth, however, when to take complete care of us and attend us constantly is to rob us of the necessary experience by which we grow, even through trial and error if we must! Tell me of a parent who can crawl or walk or reason for one of his offspring. Many try but fail miserably. And there are innumerable experiences in which the parent is helpless and must let go and let the child become!

This pattern of biological, psychological, spiritual reality is derived from the relationship originally manifest between the Creator-Parent and created-child. We cannot circumvent it!

Correct Action Leads to Self-Transformation

How, then, can we help and transform ourselves? You must actively oppose all within you which resists the truth that is telling you what you must do. There is no easy way. There is no magic formula. To go from where you are to become more like God—He who created you—you must be reformed; you must be transformed!

When you ponder within what you know you must do to transform yourself, you may become overwhelmed and so disenchanted as to give up. You must resist even this and dare to go forward, putting one foot in front of another. In so doing, you must know that you are not alone. There are those who love you and seek your freedom in God's gift of wholeness in you—they are ever surrounding you in spirit.

We would guide by example to be most direct: If you wish to transform yourself from being selfish, then you must think of and serve others. It is not enough to pray for this transformation. You draw to yourself what you are. At first, therefore, there will be resistance and therefore some uncomfortable "unnatural" feelings. You must aid yourself by visualizing yourself serving others and finding fulfillment in it. To the subconscious mind, this is like priming the pump, and makes it far easier to act with enthusiasm. When resistance arises to display itself in negative feelings and unbidden inner visualizations, do not fight it. To fight it is to feed it. Rather, displace and replace it with new visions of success.

And act even when your heart burdens you with feelings of hypocrisy. It is hypocritical only when you act without longing to truly want to change, when it is but a show. As you picture and act right feelings will follow. It is a law that as you act in accordance with truth, the right and true outcome will be manifested and you will become what you act out.

Your Life on Earth Is Very Precious

It is fortunate, blessed we should say, for you on earth to be still in the physical. We in spirit cannot act and change as we have spoken. We must return to you on earth to aid and support you; for the gift of life is your physical temple. It is by acting through the physical that the soul's vibration can be changed. When we have passed on we are devoid of this inner resonance between soul and body. Our energies are diminished and lack the power to grow closer to God.

Why do we take these hours to write and pass on this information? Because we must let you know, dear reader, how very, very precious is your life on earth. To educate and to inspire and to urge you forward we speak of the truth we know and have experienced.

Unless you reach your maximum growth on earth according to His blueprint for you, you will still have to return to earth to complete your spiritual growth. Our job is assisting others to liberate earth that through this understanding heaven may also be liberated. Though you may not understand or agree with all of our words, we would ask you to consider them!

We want again to emphasize the necessity of going against certain thoughts and feelings within you to achieve your highest good or God within! Know you are assisted at every turn! As we have said before and shall say again many times in our communication: "Think on all of this and consider what we have said."

With greatest love and respect to humankind—our brothers and sisters on earth.

Saint Germain

10:10 P.M.
July 5, 1988
West Grove, Pennsylvania

We stay on the theme of transformation. You are gradually reforming your mind, your ideas about life and yourself. It is not what you write on paper that is full reality, but what actually happens. That is life. To sit dreaming of the future without working does not cause you to live in the now. That is what we want to speak of this moment regarding your meditations and living in the now.

Do That Which Partakes of Eternity

Forget about what is to be. Hold faith in God as number one—faith that day by day you are being led. This does not mean not to plan your day. But, as you are planning, you are being guided in heart and mind on what you must do. Your own mind in its thinking process shows you priorities. Since you cannot do everything in life, you should do that which partakes of eternity. Do those things that promote the fulfillment of His ultimate work among men.

We want you to get the most from every experience and allow life to flow into your situation. You are impressed to focus and eliminate the superfluous and the extraneous. Continue to do this. Your mission in life calls for such self-discipline in order to become what heaven sees and knows you can become. Always hear that inner voice and follow it regardless of what you feel.

Be More Passive in Your Meditations

Today in meditation your mind wandered and you felt your energies scattered. We told you to be more passive, not to try too hard. We are assisting and have a road map to follow. We see your cooperation and know you are anxious. But timing is all important. So don't anticipate anything. Just be free-flowing but committed. Let each day's experience unfold as it will. Make the tape to guide yourself as you have thought. We are working to get you to that level where you routinely do the same each day, so that you are more steady. It is coming. Be very patient.

Not speed but rather depth and breadth are the important criteria for those who would do a greater than average work. As you feel called, follow and have faith in those themes that recur in your mind. These are those things that are to be fulfilled. Pursue those things that persist!

Know that when you meditate we are aware. If we are not present when you begin, we are there as you enter deeper into the meditation. You are our responsibility. We stand by at all times to serve your work. We move about you and we pass energies, personal and impersonal, on to you. We mention passive presence in you, versus active, because when you step out of the way into the more passive state we can come through to you more as we are.

All Existence Is Vibratory

Our presence is vibratory as all is vibratory. We must lower our vibration and you must raise yours. That is part of our apprenticeship together. Little by little we come closer and closer. Expectancy itself is vibratory. As you hold your expectations firm and fast, an environment is created in which we can more easily manifest.

When you enter another's home, you can sense if you are welcome in both the gestures and the facial expressions of the hosts. Beyond this outward expression is the subtle expression of feelings and attitudes (all behind the outward demonstrations). The feelings and attitudes truly manifest the real and honest atmosphere.

Your anticipation is the same. When like an innocent child you anticipate our manifestation and hold only this desire, this longing enshrouded in innocence, we can come to you easily. But doubt, fear, anxiety, and worry are vibrations also. These vibrations create an atmosphere hard to penetrate. Our love and care (not to mention our working on your mediumship) cannot mingle with vibrations slightly to extremely negative. As we have said, vibrations must be harmonious to stand side by side, to mix, or to exist together.

Is it any wonder that we find it difficult to make ourselves known broadly on earth? The vibrations surrounding earth are the cumulative vibrations of man's entire history. Have love and genuine human concern and unselfishness reigned upon the earth? No, war and more war, as an expression of the human war within, has veiled the earth in a heavy fog of negative vibrations. Not only do we feel unwelcome, we are repelled just as a man from a springboard as he jumps upon it is catapulted away from earth. It is not easy for us to come and to stay, except in an environment created consciously and unconsciously by people who are unselfish and genuine in love. With such people we find rapport and can stay longer.

The Value of Meditation Is beyond Measure

You speak on earth of raising vibrations. Yes, you need to do this and dwell in them every minute of every day, and keep them up by loving, positive, kind thoughts and deeds. Therefore, when you meditate leave all negativity outside the door. And as you meditate day after day and feel the peace resultant from such a state of mind, you will seek it again and again, and will do everything in your power to not lose it. You will become a calm in the middle of a storm; you will be an anchor on a ship in a choppy, stormy sea, a refuge for lost and frightened souls. Moreover, you will continue to draw us to you, and together we will build a spiritual edifice so high and so strong and so beautiful that nothing can penetrate it or bring it down, either on earth or in the world of spirit.

Such people leave love wherever they walk, and others are drawn to them as metal to magnet. Comfort is in their wake and solace, for they become the living personification and manifestation of Christ come to earth.

160

When you meditate, keep your innocence. However others may doubt or struggle, do not change. Do not be moved. You will see in the end how it pays off. And we will be more and more able to come into your midst to do what we are sent to do, and ultimate reality will thus be brought to earth as we work together.

Let us be as we are, and see yourself as a passageway without hindrance, without blocks. Do not anticipate every aspect of our presence or the work that we do, but leave that to us. Then we can come through so clearly. Too often mediums adopt ideas that vibrationally make it hard for us to come through unaffected by their words, their ideas. As ego dies and one trusts God-on-high and places one's very existence in His hands, then we can come to you and speak as He asks us to speak—free of prejudice and misconceptions—filled with truth as He intended and longs to convey it to His creation—man. This is His will, that all might see and know one reality as it was in the beginning!

To do this work such a state is necessary. Until tomorrow, our love and gratitude are with you in this unfolding ministry.

Those who are all for Him and His will:
Saint Germain and All

11:44 A.M.
July 6, 1988
West Grove, Pennsylvania

CHAPTER SEVENTEEN

GAINING RELEASE FROM THE PAST

Every life situation is meant to teach us something about ourselves. Each experience is a means to reflect to us who we are in character. The original essence of man would have been only good. There never should have been emotions of pain, never!

To Be Free, Let Go of the Past

You are in the midst of self-discovery. But, you must not stop with the pain that it brings. You must work positively through the pain. If you allow yourself any lesser response to this pain, you will pull yourself down and back. We have told you, and you yourself know, that the past is past. It dwells in the "now" to the degree that we allow it. It is spiritual ignorance within man that causes him to return to the past, even when it is painful. Indeed, history is itself a succession of returns to the past. Instead of learning and becoming wise, man endlessly repeats his mistakes.

Pain tells us that regardless of past events, there is need for total release of the past. There are still living, vivid emotions that pull us back and keep the past alive. We do not return to live back there when there is no emotional attachment. "Emotional" indicates a deep level of give and take with someone or something, and usually it is with someone.

These feelings, these emotions, may not be rational or justifiable; still, they are woven into our emotional network. This is vibratory and has life in itself. Our investment in past experience(s) has created this result within our spirit: what we have received as the result of our former give and take. This is true of that which is God-centered as well as all extremes, variances, and degrees away from this God-centeredness. We reap in our soul what we have sown. It is law. And you know this.

Transform and Redirect Harmful Energies

What to do with the pain? The pain is an effect and not a cause. Pain, both justifiable and unjustifiable, has resulted from the former give and take. That is, we may have derived pain from losing someone we love in death. Or we may receive pain from wrong action. Both are pain and both are resultant.

This moment, as you write, you are transforming your energies, your pain. This does not mean the pain is gone. We must recognize when we are hurting inside and not lie to ourselves by simply denying the pain. This is true with all disturbing emotions inside. It is okay to hurt and to admit to pain. A wound in the physical body may become infected and worsened unless attended to. It is the same in our spirits. But, our concern must be with the proper treatment of our internal wounds, so as not to do further damage and deepen or widen the wound.

In cases of internal wounds, resulting from having loved, there is but one ultimate cure, and that is to love again. And if the love was a misuse or improper use of your life's energies, then you must realize this, forgive, and direct your life stream to the proper use of love. There is no other way. This is transformation.

Many try simply to deny or cover up their pains from the past. Some pretend they are not there. But poison that is in the body or

163

soul must be seen for what it is and brought to the surface to be healed away, to be drawn off, to be neutralized.

Memories of painful pasts must be healed initially by accepting personal responsibility for the results in one's soul. We cannot expect anyone else to transform the negative and painful, even if it is the pain of having lost someone in death. If you don't take responsibility, who can? Even God is bound by law. He did not create you as a mechanical doll for whom He takes 100 percent responsibility.

Take Full Responsibility for Your Thoughts and Actions

Though another may be responsible for having totally or partially caused resultant pain—the pain, the vibration of pain, from painful thoughts (memories) is in you and is yours to deal with. If you make another responsible you will meet only with disillusionment, unhappiness, and despair. Only you, with God doing His portion to help, can transform a painful past into a happy present.

Whatever portion of any action resulting in unhappiness is your portion, you must take personal responsibility for that. You must not make another responsible—it can never happen.

Because man on earth has not learned from the past, he is destined to repeat the past. On the individual level, you must realize that you, in your response to all phenomena around you, are creating results according to the content of your response. Negative responses will yield more resultant negativity. As long as an inappropriate response is manifested, you are destined to repeat the past and suffer. Conversely, positive and appropriate responses bring positive results. It is the same law of cause and effect at work resulting in two different outcomes.

We define as appropriate actions those allowable within God's will or principles. Principled actions always bring happiness and peace to the soul; the opposite is true of unprincipled actions.

Practically, one must ask himself: "What thinking leads me or has led me to unhappiness?" Our appropriate or inappropriate actions are preceded by thoughts (conscious or unconscious). Our thoughts are the center and kernel of our actions. Unless we change our thoughts—the way we see, view, and/or think about any particular situation—we will continue to respond in the same way and reap the same results.

When I am out of control it means my thoughts are out of control. I am reacting, not determining or directing my mental activity. To take dominion means to stand back and look at my thoughts as factors causing me pain or joy. No one else is thinking for me. No one else is causing me to think a particular way. I alone am responsible for my own thoughts.

Overcome Obstacles by Taking Heaven's Point of View

Yes, initially in many cases our hurts are the end result of what someone has done to us. But, if you return to the past and ask for a tallying and settling of accounts, you will be disappointed. You cannot force another to say I am sorry and truly mean it. You can take responsibility only for yourself. Do not remain an emotional child crying out for someone to save you. Salvation from pain starts with new, elevated, objective, non-self-pitying, changed thinking—seeing from heaven's view.

And rather than carry a revengeful heart, simply forgive and then act anew on the base of your forgiving thoughts. This includes seeing yourself with different thoughts. Don't ever do again anything that brings pain to yourself or others. Always check your motivations, your thoughts, against the backdrop of His thought. If they are not one and the same, then you are on a path to more pain and unhappiness.

The beginning, liberating thought is: "I am responsible and I can be responsible." We are at the mercy of caprice or whim only so long as we think we are. And even in situations where we are shackled and cannot immediately move up in life, we can be elevated, even in the midst of the worst pain, the worst squalor, by changing our thinking, not to thoughts of slavish acceptance or passivity but to constructive thoughts of upliftment, hope, love, forgiveness. In the end of life's journey, it is the human soul that must be able to rise to His presence immediately upon departure from earth, life's circumstances notwithstanding.

Many have suffered through deprivation and have come to bless their circumstances, even when far from ideal. These have been immediately elevated to the highest realms of spirit because they lived with heavenly thoughts regardless of their surroundings. Their thoughts transcended the earth and brought to them results in kind. Heaven began in their thoughts—the way they viewed and responded to life's circumstances—and before they left the earth plane they were already dwelling in the land of loving, God-infused thoughts.

Take your time and work through your thoughts carefully. Protect yourself and thus others as well from repeating the thoughts and resultant actions that lead to inappropriate manifestations and pain.

Take personal responsibility, then heaven can help you, for taking personal responsibility is within the "laws of life" and provides the needed base for Him and us to help you help yourself. Take responsibility and become truly free.

Saint Germain

4:23 A.M.
July 10, 1988
West Grove, Pennsylvania

Forgiveness and repentance always have to do with changing our thoughts. Transformation is the process of changing our old, inappropriate ways of thinking into new ways—new thoughts.

Confession, Repentance, Forgiveness, Are Means, Not Ends

Forgiveness, confession, repentance bring before us our old thoughts, our misguided, misdirected thoughts. These actions cause us to examine and bring to the surface those thoughts that keep us on the treadmill of resultant unhappiness and pain.

The emphasis should always be upon reforming and thus transforming our thought energies to God-centered, God-motivated thoughts. Forgiveness, confession, and repentance are means, not ends. Many become stuck in confession and repentance. To simply tell someone what we have done wrong and to say we will turn away from it is just the beginning.

By confessing you draw the poisons of your soul to the surface. Once they are before your eyes you need not continue to confess but seek always to place your energies upon developing new thoughts that will lead you to new actions and happiness.

By repenting you are apologizing and telling what thoughts leading to correspondent actions you are turning away from. Then establish new ways of thinking, again we say, to lead you to appropriate God-centered actions from which repenting will not be necessary.

New Thinking, New Action, Leads to Transformation

It is new thinking we must be absorbed in, not repenting, confessing. There are times when we need to repent for something over and over because we ourselves have not realized the weight nor the fullness of our erroneous thoughts. This repentance by repetition clarifies. But only as certain thoughts and resultant actions repeat themselves would we continue to repent.

Some make repentance an end in itself. Gone are those days as a mode of ongoing action. We know through working with modern scientific studies that energy can neither be created nor destroyed but only transformed. Our thoughts are the energy behind the actions of our lives. If we want to "act" differently in accordance with His will and constructive ends, then we must transform our thoughts.

Forgiveness—while in a different category than repentance and confession—has to do with transformation. To forgive others or ourselves places positive thoughts in our mind about others or ourselves and changes our thoughts so as to see others and ourselves in positive terms, positive light. This releases us from restrictive, negative mental energies and frees "us" and "them" from unhappiness. When you forgive and truly forgive, even if it is "seventy times seventy," you are transforming your own thoughts and creating freedom for yourself. This is taking responsibility.

No matter what, we must approach all of life's circumstances with a positive mind. Out of such energies can life's situations be transformed. Moreover, we have then the energies to do the transforming. Positive energy brings upliftment and freedom in the soul. Conversely, negative energy suppresses, depresses, and restricts. Go with the positive, go with the positive, go with the positive! And be reborn, be transformed!

Saint Germain

7:21 A.M.
August 10, 1988
Riverdale, Maryland

CHAPTER EIGHTEEN

THE CLEANSING POWER OF TRUTH

With every problem there is a solution. With every experience there is a lesson to be learned, not just intellectualized but acted upon to overcome and go higher. Don't concern yourself with where these thoughts come from. Truth is truth no matter whether from your own understanding or from one of us outside of yourself. And if we all follow ultimate truth, we cannot help but be united on every level in this work.

God Is the Only Reality

We want you to refrain from thinking of us here and you there. There is no separation internally. Spirit world is the world of heart where what you think and feel is also what you are. There can be no illusions here unless you *choose* to accept the illusions as fact, and then for you that illusion becomes reality.

It is not different on earth. How many, believing that they are right, are willing even to die for their cause? Religious zealots, politicians, people of all kinds of ideologies propound their mental wares as absolute fact. It is an illusion and it has power to cause people to act because they cannot see otherwise. There is only one fact in the world and that is God! Only those lives lived totally according to the ultimate truth of life have substance. All else is illusion. That truth comes from the mind of God Himself. Life as He envisioned it is ultimate reality. That vision has never changed, never once! All the illusions of man, all the half-truths and "derivative-isms" in life, have derailed him and sent him down pathways to disillusion. Over and over has man thwarted God's grand vision.

None of us has known this fully. And so the plight of human history is suffering. You cannot follow that which is partially true and be either successful or happy. None—including God—has ever been truly happy, because His ideal, His grand vision, has not been realized.

Awaken from False and Hypnotic Illusions

But, mankind continues to suffer because mankind has not awakened from the hypnotic power of illusions—visions of false grandeur and false happiness. Men go on cranking out unhappiness for themselves and others. We all suffer from each others' misuse of energy.

Look at the world around you and see the misused energies. See them reflected in everyday tragedies from individual battles, suffering and struggles, to all-out war. This is not the world the Creator, in all His love and truth, had in mind. Even He is alienated from earth, while at the same time bound to earth by cords of compassion and love. Worse still, even He is overwhelmed by "what man hath wrought" upon this planet. Even He is frightened for man. Because until enough men and women on earth realize earth's future lies in *their* hands, He cannot act. He cannot remold man in a moment, nor undo the historical tragedies in a twinkling of the eye. Man must reverse his course. He cannot simply create a new and better world upon the trash heap of yesteryear's failures.

Man must clean up the earth physically and spiritually. And he must cleanse himself and create a new world order. Mankind in mutual cooperation must do this. We need such men and women.

Repentance Cleanses the Debris of the Heart

The formula we have imparted here applies not only to Mother Earth and her children collectively, but also to each of us individually. We purposely include the word "us" for we in spirit are bound to this earth to help clean it and its inhabitants. For it is mankind's past and present cumulative misuse of His energy that has seeped into and poisoned not only the earth, but man himself.

The formula indicates that you cannot simply expect to push away all of your misdeeds and their resultant energies and be free and born anew. Each of you too must dig deep into the soil of yourselves—and we mean this word to have actual meaning—and you must cleanse yourselves as well as create a new you.

You cannot simply step over your misuse of energy and expect it not to resurface somewhere from underneath the soil of your heart. Repentance is that action which burns up and cleans up the debris you thought you had left behind and covered up. You must see these things within yourself and confess them so that together you, we, and God can purge you of the old and unwanted. To try to cover it all up with pretense to peace and happiness is begging for trouble—just as while a body can appear entirely healthy it can, at the same time, be filled with cancer.

We do not speak lightly of all of this, nor are we interested in the beauty of our commentary. What we have said is truth. It may cause difficulty. If it does so to the point it makes you love yourselves more, seeing your inner realities and working system-atically to change, then so be it!

In the end, these words are not of accusation but of love. Some of you want freedom from all pain. But, truthfully, you are all suffering from spiritual, inherited diseases. We can give you a sugar coated pill "to make the medicine go down in a most delightful way," but it is unrealistic. We do that usually to shield you from too much too soon. But our message today is not for that purpose.

The power of the truth must do its internal work to cleanse you. This starts in the mind. We seek to impress your mind by some relatively jarring frankness so that a kind of crisis is created to cause you to sense an emergency and move toward quick and decisive action.

Pursue Only Eternal Values

The problem is illusions. Because you cannot see beyond what your physical life has shown you, you do not see at all or at least very little of the true effects of the misaligned causes within your soul. And you perceive incorrectly that you have plenty of time, and think that tomorrow will be soon enough to change or act. Time is a thief. And it speeds by faster than you perceive.

In his illusions, man uses his time here on earth for strictly material/physical purposes. He indulges in activities that do indeed have their consequences in spirit, but he is not bothered because he does not see their results—otherwise he would be shocked and ashamed! He carries upon his own soul, upon his own spirit-face, upon his own spirit-body, and within his total spiritual energies the scars, the marks, the distortions and twistedness of all of his misdeeds on earth. This is frightening to behold in spirit and at its extreme is absolutely repulsive.

We weep to see man's ignorance of these ultimate realities. No one is free of consequences. "What you sow, you also reap." And everyone has distortions in their perceptions of reality. Consequently, we are not speaking to a few dregs of the earth as those who consider themselves above all this might think. No, we speak to all humanity. All humanity. There are no exceptions.

After you realize your inner self, act quickly to clean it up, to get rid of the old by dealing with it. In spiritual terms we first see our wrongs, our twisted natures. Then we voice them in enumerating them before heaven, and we seek to give them up and turn them over by a contrite heart and determination not to redo the wrongs, *not even to dwell on them*. This we call the act of repentance: to "turn away from."

Transformation: the Result of Acting According to Truth

Now begins the real work: to act according to truth and to be so imbued with truth and truthfulness that we can't help but act in accordance with it regardless of our feelings. You must now visualize the new you. You must animate it with life, with breath, and you must bring it into existence through the proper use of your life energies—this we call *acting* in accordance with the truth irrespective of feelings. This act we call "transformation."

You must transform your life. You must become master of your energies in accordance with God's will. Love is the igniter of this action and the fuel that keeps the flame of desire to transform alive. But, due to distortions in love and wrong perceptions, we must also direct our love according to God's will or God's truth. To those who think of love in romantic, poetic, or sweet terms, this may seem cold. But, from a higher level as seen by us, love is an energy, a vibration within your soul and it too must be directed and managed. Otherwise, it can and often does direct and manage your reasoning mind. This is backwards. Love is truly sweet when it is elevated to the highest level. But, on the way it can be our enemy until we have understood the emotions of love and mastered them. You all know the truth that we speak by your life experiences—you are endowed with love through His gift in you. But, it is not to be wasted or misused, or it will be turned from a gift that brings joy and eternal happiness to a curse that brings endless sorrow.

Become Master of Your Feelings

We close with feelings. Do not trust them until you are master over them. By that time you will know yourself and what you can and cannot trust in your feelings. Until humanity is elevated back to the very heart of God—cemented in its center and He in the center of their hearts—man cannot trust his feelings to be objective, true, or principled. If we all were to do just what we feel, we would be animals. And the lowest realms of this world of spirit are populated with those who lived according to their feelings and did what their feelings led them to do. They are suffering the consequences of such a loose and animal life by living in the form of an animal. It is more than appalling to behold.

Make gods of no one, nor of any man-made ideas. Seek *the* God of this life and all life and raise your being to Him day after day. This and this alone will dispel illusions, raise the mind to its proper level, and cleanse the heart in the soil of the human soul. Turn from the past and transform your energies into pure white light. Then take your seat among the few who have dared to live a life on earth so as to receive joy eternal!

This message comes from a conglomerate source as we all

surround you to impart our universal, timeless energy and messages.

With His Greatest Love and Truth

12:30 P.M.
July 14, 1988
West Grove, Pennsylvania

CHAPTER NINETEEN

THE IMPORTANCE OF ACTIVELY SEEKING

Sometimes it takes extremes to teach us what is valuable in life. And though you may hurt, this hurt will cause you to seek a solution to your life's needs.

We respect your needs and understand your struggles. We continue to be there, for true love is not conditional. Now you can break the bonds with the past and soar aloft to your ultimate abode with Him. Know this is in the offing and don't believe or think otherwise.

God's Love Is Unchanging and Unconditional

Time has passed and we have been apart too long—you and I. But, always when separate (though I never separate myself from you) we grow wiser through our realizations of value, true value. God is not fickle, to simply cast aside value to be redeemed. And you may think you can influence this writing experience to say what you want or need it to say, but the reality is that God is ever there and unchanging. And we lead you—even if by a sad and tear-stained, sodden path—to be unchanging too. And you are becoming so.

And why, when you fail or draw back from our mutual purpose together, do we not punish you? Because we need not do that.

Your conscience makes you responsible and is a merciless taskmaster. But even its purpose in its original design is to serve as a guidance system to lead you back, even by difficult ways, to Him. And so in its gentle and harsh ways it parents us to our highest good!

Also, from our perspective we know you have punished yourself in many ways already. And you have learned well that it serves no purpose but to hold you back. Old and primitive ways of seeking to stimulate soul growth are outmoded and stifle the soul from growth. It is best to acknowledge our wrongs and use our energies to correct them, not dwell upon them.

Correct Self-Love Is the Path to Liberation

For those with revengeful, primitive minds and hearts, crude punishment seems justified. But it has never worked, ultimately. To be saved, a soul needs to know that wrong is wrong, and if he does wrong he shall suffer by the working of universal law—sowing and reaping. But a soul who does wrong does so because he does not truly love himself. He may be driven by this reality to punish himself unconsciously. His mind is twisted, and he wavers back and forth until at last he sees reality. Enough pain in life tells him he must be doing something wrong.

Our love is redemptive. And though we may withhold it for a while to teach through our absence that true love is the only path to our higher selves, permanent withholding would be destructive.

Often it is when spiritual help appears to be removed from man that he more strongly seeks God, the ultimate and consummate goal of life.

There is cause and effect in all of life's working out. And yes, an effect can become a cause. Because of some outcome (effect) in life we may make changes and act differently. God is wise in using the result to man's positive advantage and so teaches us. This is universal, ultimate reality.

So wherever a soul may be in its journey upward from darkness into light, it is on the path to salvation. There are no exceptions to this reality. And one by one God, through all diverse circumstances, is reaching out his arms to each soul. Many do not know this and spend most of their lives floundering just to exist. But He will never abandon one soul, for that soul is His child. That child is the end result of a creative process that He put into existence and motion. He is responsible, and love's lure cannot let Him escape from that which He designed and placed in the cosmos. He is responsible: "I have purposed . . . I will fulfill all!"

Place Yourself under God's Umbrella of Love

For God, it is not a question of whether He shall stand at our side or not. Rather, the question is: will man see Him there? Usually not. We of spirit testify that we are here and shall remain for the single purpose of serving His cause to save mankind. And though diverse approaches have been used to do so, our ends are the same: to place His child back fully into His care and under His umbrella of love. That is the sole and central purpose which we serve.

From afar we may seem independent and unconnected to any whole. However, if you could see it close up, you would see the network of His love and guidance that works to bring us into one end. We know this in the highest levels of spirit world. From our vantage point there can be no question. We are here because we sought His will above our own and discovered that will. His ultimate purpose in all of life's unfolding on planet earth and in spirit is salvation! Salvation! Salvation! To save us from the world of pain caused by the misuse of His energies. Therefore, He teaches and teaches us—meaning all mankind—His ways. And in eternal patience He endures to the end.

Precious is each soul to Him and to us. We can see now as He sees. His tears have become our tears, His grief our grief, His sadness and despair our sadness and despair. While we hide this from the world at large and continue to encourage poor, struggling humanity, our hearts ache over the reality of man's plight. But, while we withdraw from time to time to allow man to learn through suffering, we shall never give up! When you truly, truly love as He does, you can't give up. We cannot forget man's cry for spiritual help even when it is but a faint sound in the soul's heart. We return again and again to planet earth to do our work.

Climb the Ladder of Spiritual Evolution

When one seeks as you are seeking, we draw nearer than ever. We cling tenaciously to such people. But so do lower forces. And such people at times become a center of raging mental war. We work to guarantee that with the proper merit and potential you cannot fail!

So few and far between are those who seek Him. Many follow *form*, and it is one of the rungs on the ladder of the evolution of the human soul. But, it is not a high rung. It is *love* of which life is composed at the core. And love's call from inside the soul is the last and highest rung on the ladder of spiritual evolution.

We seek those who understand from love's point of view why they must seek God—a true and living experience with the LIVING GOD! Only love can do that. Only love can draw man, compel man to come to his highest self. And only the love experience with God can do this! Many experience His love. But like small children, they are satisfied to take it and take it without knowing the real truths of His heart and mind—of His suffering;

that He has been hurt in love beyond man's comprehension. That He has loved ceaselessly from the beginning of man's creation and literally poured forth all that He has and is to love man. Who returned this love? Yes, some realized a portion and offered thanks. But who among billions of souls has known the true degree and depth with which He has loved us?

There is no substitute for His love, none! And man cannot live, truly live, without it. Man is, therefore, destined one day to meet this love full force. And God has willed it so. He has but one will when it comes to love, and that is to love until *all* have returned to Him!

Saint Germain

6:23A.M.
August 16, 1988
West Grove, Pennsylvania

CHAPTER TWENTY

CHARACTER, REPETITION, AND THE LABOR OF LOVE

We have called you again to rise and go forward: to recreate wholeness of thought which descends into the soul and body to make them whole as well. There remain topics yet to cover or to finish, and today is the day to do so. Together we recreate ourselves and realign ourselves with each other. We surround you with our abiding love.

The Pictures in Your Mind Are Powerful

Often, as you have just thought, we come to you in pictures. Your ear does not hear a voice, but your mind sees and captures an image or picture. This we have chosen to call "picture power." Just now, as you wrote, a picture of an audience viewing a slide show appeared before your inner eye. And with that picture you also saw amplifications and changes. This is our influence. This is our direct bearing upon the screen of your mind. It is here too that He speaks and guides you. And as is so often said, "a picture is worth a thousand words." It is simpler and easier for us to speak so and much faster. Watch for more unfolding in this way.

Back to the slide show and "picture power." Those pictures that appear before the audience can lull them into slumber or cause them to rise to excitement. So significant is a picture—even without words!

The pictures of life and self bear predominantly upon the soul in its unfolding. What pictures dominate your life? Find this and you will find your enemy and/or your friend. Only in recent years has man discovered the power of pictures of the mind in the West. In the East it is so ingrained that they take it for granted. From this inner window of the soul is intuition wrought. Even the Eastern languages have their derivation in pictures, thus making their language expression quite literal and much easier to learn.

Pictures and Symbols Are the Language of Spirit

Jesus spoke in pictures too. More than tradition, it was the means of expression in his time and culture. In the sophisticated world of today those pictorial expressions are thought by some to be primitive and archaic. We, however, say that they are vital and primary to humanity's reawakening.

In our world of spirit often—more often than not—our expressions to each other are the pictures in our minds. And you have been told that this age will be highly philosophical and filled with symbolism. What is a symbol but a picture expressed in simplified terms—a message in pictorial form.

Our two worlds are coming together to be eventually one world. If man on earth is ever fully and universally to awaken to the world of cause, then he must be instructed, be prepared to make this breakthrough, by beginning to think symbolically, pictorially. The current emphasis upon inner visualization and meditation especially in the Western world has come to bridge the distance between East and West, and between the spirit world and earth.

With this growing interest and emphasis it is easier and easier for us in spirit to touch earth with affection and images so as to lead earth to heaven. This emphasis and practice is heralding the way to enlightenment and easing our interaction with all mankind on earth.

Holy Scriptures Paint Visions of Man's Higher Self

All written words create pictures in the mind of man. Down through the ages sages, wise men, rabbis, and ministers alike have emphasized the power of the written word. Why? Though there are many "isms" in religion and theology, all impact similarly upon the mind of man. That is, they create in him new mental pictures, causing him to see differently from inside and thus to act differently in the physical. When touched by the finger of God's divinity, it is true that new emotions arise, but there emerges as well a new image of self deep within the soul's mind. And it is the new emotions that create pictures of hope and joy and new actions in the unfolding life of the person so touched. In spirit, we seldom say, "I love you." First, we know by actions that we are loved and are secure in this. Secondly, we can see the picture of love coming from any soul and can feel it easily, for it is not only pictorial but also vibratory.

In the West you often say "I love you" out of habit, obligation, and desire. But actions say, "I love you," not words. If you were more attuned as a people you would know deep inside that you are loved or not loved and cease from saying so often and unnecessarily, "I love you." If your inheritance of heart were based upon a tradition of loving by action and withholding words, your heart, your sensing faculties of heart would grow. Under such circumstances words are superfluous. Think on this and see if this is not a major and basic difference between East and West. Neither sphere of the two hemispheres is perfect, but certainly the East leads the West on this point.

Let us return to religious teachings and the written word. As you read any works in the religious field, you are led to paths and pastures of character. Over and over, are depicted values and virtues of a raised, purified, and holy life dedicated to a Supreme Being. How does this affect the mind and heart of man? By consistent exposure to such writings, man begins to create an opening in his heart for God to enter and to affect qualitatively his heart and thereby his thinking. These precious works handed down from age to age have each done their part to raise man to a higher level, though there is still a ways to go.

Aspire to Grow by Emulating the Spiritual Masters

Man has caught an inner vision—a series of connected pictures—that lifts his mind to see himself on a higher, more noble plane. And for those who return again and again to these sources, spending time among those of the same common practice, gradually, little by little, the inner images derived from scriptures become a reality within the soul and life of the disciple.

Who can read the life of Jesus or Paul in Christian scripture and not be touched, seeing mental pictures of these giants of faith? And in so doing, who would not long to emulate this faith—to catch a vision of themselves doing the same—seeking the holy and higher life? In this way God and spirit lead man on and on.

To say all of this is not to detract from the other aspects of such writings such as literary quality or tradition or history. But none of these things are ends in themselves! All are but means to the end of man's changing ever more into the image of God! History has told us who, how, why, and where. But the end must be to bring man back to God. This is the ultimate end: that love's call can be fulfilled between Creator and created.

The Value of Repetition in Achieving Spiritual Goals

Now we want to speak on the need for repeating and repeating so that the inner pictures can dawn fully and completely into the external life of man. Today's world is so confused as to where it is going. Many disdain traditions, family, marriage, child bearing, child raising, work, responsibilities to friends and relatives, affection to proper others. Our list could go on and on. Man, away from God the Father, has lost his way in the meaning and purpose of life!

Life is simple and is given to teach us many necessary lessons by which we can grow and raise our spirits to God. Have you ever noticed how many things of life are repetitious and universal? Is this accidental? All things that exist naturally are created by God for their form *and* their content—for their practical, useful function and their beauty. So it is with many and most daily tasks in life around the world. How many times in your life do you rise from sleep to follow the multitude of daily repetitive activities? You cannot count them!

God's Eternal Labor of Love Maintains All Life

The heart beats endlessly and repetitively from birth to departure from earth. Its rhythmic pulse of ebb and flow carries life to every cell of the body. Its function is to beat endlessly to carry food to each cell that the whole can be served. The heart is so loyal and sacrificial. Other organs may rest, but not brother heart. Tirelessly he toils twenty-four hours per day! Do you love this organ that keeps you alive even while "you" sleep, mindless of its labors of love? Would you be a heart to serve this endless way, never having a vacation, never a break from labor? For this "heart" was created and finds fulfillment in this role. It was indeed created to go without ceasing. Without its continuously repeated tasks man's physical life ceases. So many lessons to learn from brother heart! We should bow low before such dedication.

Deeper still is the lesson of God's untiring labor in love for man. Does He ever sleep or rest from his care of his child? Does He not walk on and on to find us and call out to us? Is He not ever watchful over every soul? Is He not the Heart of the heart of man? Is it not His hidden beat behind the beat of our own heart that maintains life? Yes, it is! Praise God and His heart in our heart!

Let us speak further on those things we do daily throughout life. Have you ever tried to stop thinking? It is impossible because the mind never rests from its watchtower of overseeing the body and soul. Even in sleep you hear, in your dreams and even in the deepest stillness of your sleep, "someone" inside is listening to answer the call to awaken. If no one were listening why did you answer the call to rise? You were not in some blank and trance state where no intelligence was on duty. No, your inner, inner mind is ever responsible because it is connected to the mind of God! And He never sleeps and is ever on watch in each of His children. He never sleeps. Do you appreciate brother brain/mind/intelligence? We should bow low before our mind in gratitude and joy for its constant attendance of our entire being. Mind is the divinity in man that never sleeps. Day after day mind serves over the endless small and large responsibilities of God's charge, man!

Your Body Serves You Tirelessly

Day after day the organs of respiration, digestion, excretion function silently inside the body. Whatever they are asked to do, they do their best, even when man abuses them. It is their function and labor of love and consequently their beauty to do as they do. Over and over, day after day, month after month, year after year they do their job. A thankless job. How humble and simple in faith would they be if they were human! Blessed are they in their gift of functioning as they do to give and maintain life, even when man never gives a care or thought to their repetitious and unending task. Whether man is asleep or awake, they do their job. The energies of life keep them ever at work doing what they do. Let us bow in heart to these gifts of life and learn their lesson.

In concert do our hands, feet, arms, legs, eyes, nose, touch, hearing, and tasting work externally to give us contact with the external life. When you abuse any of them or those internally functioning organs, they will rebel by law against that abuse. Under normal circumstances they work day by day fulfilling responsibilities. We must love and cherish them all, bowing low in heart to their service to us. And remember the lessons they teach us about ourselves and the instructions they impart through their day-by-day, on-the-job functioning. And together in them we will find God!

Repetitious Tasks Maintain Families and Societies

In the care of a child is the lesson of love. A mother cannot remember the number of times she changes her child's diaper. It is a task done so often without thought. It seems meaningless and inconsequential. But it is not. How does He care for us? Is He not ever near to hear us cry our many needs? And does He not endlessly clean up the messes we have made of our lives? Indeed, His is a mother's and father's heart!

The helpless child God created must have a serving and caring parent. A bond forms and love grows through continuous parental service in raising the child. The animal kingdom is not truly a kingdom of love, though it may reflect degrees of love. There are attachments and there is dedication through which a bond is formed. This ensures the successful nurturing, protection, and raising of the young. However, animals cannot distill lessons of life from their instinctive functions to the degree that humans can. Instinct was simply God's way of providing for animal survival. But as man observes the animal kingdom he can more deeply understand himself, others, and God.

Traditionally, it has been the father who leaves the home to work and provide income for the family. Countless are the men of history who have done so while traditionally the wife maintained the home. Day after day he rose to go to the workplace to perform repetitious tasks of some kind of mental or physical labor for an income. As they worked, most thought of their family and future. And this is still so. Without dedication to the purpose of the family through repetition, families and societies could never maintain themselves.

This labor of love repeated often for decades and decades within an individual husband's life caused him to be the center and pillar of the family whom everyone in the family looks up to. And it teaches the man love in action, or the command of love, which is responsibility.

A deeper lesson for mankind lies in the example of the ever-present protection and provision possible through the father of a family. In such a family it is easy to explain God and create inner images in the minds of all as to who and what God is, especially as you put mother and father in their inner and outer functions and responsibilities together—as repetitious as they may be.

Love Transforms Drudgery into Self-Realization

God is ever concerned, ever providing for man's inner and outer life. He works repetitiously at His labor of love, continuously acting to raise man back to Him, no matter how long He must labor, even eons of time. In all of this experience of repetition man can find his true self. As mundane, as seemingly simple, as boring as life may seem, if it is connected repetitiously and consistently to God it is all worth it. What was drudgery is now a labor of love, even if done 365 days per year for 100 years of life.

We want also to discuss repetitive expression of love or affection. We all need such love. Love is not a static thing, but is to be experienced over and over because God in His love and wisdom made man so, because He is so! He ever and ever needs our love through loyalty and praise, worship, understanding, affection, and dedication. He needs our comfort, too.

It is the soul's God-given emptiness needing refilling from time to time that causes us to repeat our loving acts to others and they to us. It is not a mere physical act to love another.

Praise for the common art of which life is built! Praise for life patterns that are good! And praise for the repetition that gives them meaning, teaches us, and raises us to Him!

Saint Germain and Band

10:32 A.M.
August 16, 1988
West Grove, Pennsylvania

Part Five
God, Christ and
Spiritual Transformation

CHAPTER TWENTY-ONE

CHRIST-CONSCIOUSNESS

Yes, it is I [Saint Germain]. I was deeply moved by your prayer this morning. We gathered and will continue to gather as you and your family pray. Your prayer is our food and salvation. Please continue. The cumulative effect of prayer is important. The vital points you pray about are important, lodge in the heart and mind, and influence for eternity.

When you write, write more slowly. It is not necessary to race ahead. I am with you as I have led you to be in this work. Be patient and quiet in yourself. Work this way and move forward wisely and smoothly.

In Times of Crisis, Focus on Priorities

We know that you have been troubled by several things this week. You have thought this to be one of the worst weeks of your life. This may be so because the issue of life and death loomed in your mind. Oh, so many things had to be considered, didn't they? You quickly decided what was priority and what was superfluous. You had to think deeply about the condition of your soul and the souls of those who are your responsibility. More than this, you came to know your weaknesses. Despair hung heavy in your heart. A great lesson of true life came your way, didn't it? This was so important. From this experience you can have gratitude, and the understanding to go on.

Today there is no pain in your body. We want to tell you that the origin of this pain began in the spiritual and manifested in the nerves of your body. It was important, as self-centered as it made you, to go through this. You have gained release and you will continue to reflect and grow from this. Never take the body for granted, thank Him daily for this abode—guard it as sacred. There were a number of reasons for this "attack." That is over now—move on and up. Can you still love after this?

Don't you see that while you aspire to mediumship, we are preparing you for only the best and nothing less? To do your best, you must walk with God every minute of every day. *This is Christ-consciousness!*

Christ-Consciousness Is Awareness of God within Us

We of this level of mind are not fanatics who spout truth all day and judge people. Rather, we move and have our existence in the total awareness of God within us. We have cleared the passageway by the same kind of struggling and overcoming that you have passed through and are passing through. We have cleared our internal, spiritual passageway of self. We think from a "we" perspective. In this, each of us finds wholeness, power, love, and joy. We do not mind, nor are we aware of giving up self. Our "self" is God's illumination of our minds and the total manifestation of His heart and mind within us.

To be Christ-conscious means to be more aware of Him and His will, than ours. In living this way, we want for nothing. God's love is complete in the center of the center of man. Jesus knew this by direct experience, and could act in no way other than as he did. He had a choice and he could see the possibilities. But, because he loved that which he experienced and was in God, love caused him to have really only one choice.

This choice ultimately was not hard for him to make. The consequences of his choice were of no concern to him. Not only did he know and embody his love experience with his Father, he also was open and knew directly the existence of spirit. He saw cause and effect firsthand. He didn't read it and receive it vicariously; he knew by hands-on experience. There was no room for doubt. Faltering was not a possibility for him. The cross was ultimately no obstacle to his existence. Weak in flesh and vulnerable was he, as all mortal men would be. But in his thoughts and feelings he was already aflame. He returned immortal, to lead as he had been led. And that is all history.

The Greatest Central Truth: God Is!

The men of faith who contributed the most in history walked the way of life with God in reality. They were more than spiritually open, and had more than mere dreams and visions. They also had more than superficial, external contact with spirit. They were alive from within, because they had been touched by the highest of highest spirits—God Himself. This could not be stopped.

You must link your awareness and that of others to the Cause behind all spiritual phenomena, that the "rank and file" of heaven are lined up, according to love and truth. The highest truth is that "God Is," and that "He Is love," and from this great truth descends all other truths and all other lesser loves. For this reason the I AM work I have done before means God Is. This has been and is still the one great tenet, teaching, truth of my leading, my ultimate prompting.

When one knows by experience that God IS, there is no other *more* important thing, no higher Truth! To say the great I AM is in me, is to say the second great truth: God Is, I therefore AM! This is the highest mathematical equation there is. He is one and He is one in me! And in this way, through each of us, He multiplies Himself. There is no greater central, single truth than God Is!

When we *know* this, we have reached the end of our searching and have but to deduct the consequences, the commandments, the dictates, the blessings, from this truth, in order to know how to be whole and how to live. This *is* Christ-consciousness. This is man fully alive when knowing and living this greatest of truths. This is the man whom you call Jesus, and this is what made him *Christ*. We are all Christ when we have understood and lived this reality. This is, and was, Jesus' central truth, central message. God Is! It is the absolute of his existence and ours too. Once we know and we know that we know, then we must seek and understand exactly how to live according to this awareness.

Christ-consciousness has become a catch-all phrase in metaphysical circles. It, like so many truths, has become abstract, meaningless, and without power. But in its original meaning it is simple but great, and therefore powerful. Christ was aware of the God of the universe—internally and externally. This awareness is the beginning and essence of Christ-consciousness.

This is my admonition for today. I gladly, joyously, celebrate this great truth above all and commend it to you as a point to *always* ponder, *always* meditate on, and *always* live. Philip, few have grasped this real essence of my teachings. My words were simple and basic, but have become meaningless through metaphysical mumbo-jumbo. Man's pseudo-pride has made it so. I am pleased to come through to clarify my real intent, my real drive which is world restoration. We understood and understand this well. It all began eons ago. Your day is the day of reaping what we have sown, whatever name you call it.

When Anchored in God, You Will Find Consistency Within

You have been impressed with many topics. You can influence the choice by ego interference. We cannot cover everything in one sitting. Nor do we want to. Rather, with the limitations of time we must impress you with the thoughts of highest and farthest reaching value. You will learn as you write. Yours is a dual experience: the first is learning to be a good instrument for us. And second, you must study and learn from the truths that we bring through your mediumship. You are most fortunate because you can not only experience our presence firsthand but can also acquire invaluable knowledge.

You feel this morning that I am different. While, like yourself, I can display the full array of human emotions if and when needed, I am never overcome by great fluctuations in my feelings as manifested in moodiness. I am steadfast in my purpose and not moved or swayed by subjective awareness. If you are consistently moved by the spirit of God, mood swings are almost non-existent. Such emotional volatility is more a thing of the earth plane where few understand or embrace an eternal purpose. Lacking this knowledge and dedication, they also lack a strong will to act with consistency. Thus the awareness of most individuals changes from day to day, resulting in multiple emotional ups and downs and a scattering of precious human energies.

Essentially I never change because I know my eternal purpose and therefore my daily duties. This results in absolute security at all times. My core energies, like those of the Father whom I serve, are peace and bliss itself. Anchored in God as I am, I ride upon the waters of His wisdom and bask in the sunlight of His love. Under such conditions how can I not be totally secure and consistent in all that I do?

We Are Sensitive to Your Time and Energy Limits

What you are sensing this morning about me stems from your own growth and awareness. You are experiencing other dimensions of me that you have not experienced before. This however, is not because I am different but because *you* are different. Your state of mind is expanded, allowing you to experience me in greater depth and in this way I only appear, from your side, to be different. As you remain steadfast in your upward climb to spiritual maturity, you will continue to expand. You shall experience all of life from a deeper and higher perspective. This includes not only God, me, and all of those who guide and work with you, but also yourself. This is what self-realization is all about. By the way, for our purposes, we would not have you totally entranced, for while you receive to help others by sharing what we give, we are also raising you. For this purpose it is important that you be fully awake and fully aware.

And while we work with you, because this is a cooperative effort, you must exercise discretion regarding our occupation of your time. We know how dedicated you are to complete your mission. Indeed, we share that dedication. But neither of us should ever lose sight of practical limitations and the necessity of doing things in such a way that no harm comes to you either spiritually or physically. We all know how demanding true mediumship is. In our zeal, however, we may forget from time to time and over-tax you. We respect your energies and need your help, now and again, to prevent our over-using you.

Write on as you have, and I will lead you by direct words and subtleties. I want you to refrain from looking back at your writing, in order to demonstrate trust. This vibration ranks high in the array of human states of mind. I can come in on it with a greater strength than if you look logically, intellectually at what you have written. There is greater purity retained when you don't retrace my words. I am aware of phrasing, transitions, and endings. Let me handle that, not to be dominating, but to teach you to trust yourself and through this to trust me.

Factors That Influence Correct Spiritual Understanding

Back to the above topics: Yes, I use your memory. Yes, I use the full accouterment of your mental, emotional power. It is this present and cumulative power—stored energy held within the confines of your being—to which I am drawn and which enables me to come to you.

So if you need information stored in your mental library to draw upon, I will cause you to reflect. Why not? It is natural in this fully awake state. We will use the full array of mental and emotional powers within you to reach you and others. God usually speaks to man through himself. We, in spirit, use these same powers and often are the means for Him to speak to man.

Stand by and relax.

We wanted to address your pondering about mediums and their means, ways, and clarity in receiving. You must always be aware that man on earth, whether he knows it or not, is in control.

We may overshadow him, but we do not take him over. We can never simply remove the remaining consciousness of a man even when entranced and he is "earthly miles" from the body. No, we are limited by what and who such a person is in his daily existence.

Purity of Love and Purity of Motive Are Most Important

The purity we look for from the lofty levels of spirit is purity in love—not always the way that it is practiced, but if it is selfless. Sometimes victims of life practice selfless love in an illicit way. But that center, that motive is pure and can be used to lead that person to God's love. Having served another or others selflessly, and having done it in a pure and balanced way, when turned, that person will be as devoted and selfless in his love toward God. We can use this. You cannot discern this point on earth so easily. We can, because heart-motive shines brighter here than anything else.

One may pretend and appear as a bright light, but the center is dark because motive is impure—mostly selfish and corrupt.

Be discerning always about mediums. Do not judge them on character alone, nor demonstration alone, but rather see how God will use them by discerning their love. If love for others is truly lacking and true love is feigned, know that he or she may indeed be a telephone between two worlds—but act and respond cautiously regarding information coming from them and/or their guides.

There are countless unprincipled spirits here. They have their corresponding counterparts in mediums on earth. You will meet them on the way to your goals. It is a good rule of thumb for you to observe in yourself, "Do I love from a selfless standpoint?" If you do, you will move many hearts and bring them closer to our reality and His reality, the reality of God—He who has sent us. This *is* the essence, the center of your work. Unless this principled point is taken, you will be just like the majority. Much to share but little to move. These are all things you are adding to your cumulative knowledge.

You are tiring and under such conditions it is harder to come through. Rest, and if you feel our prompting later in the day to write, do so. I am always pleased to come through as we grow in this work together. While it may seem you have to cross many difficult places alone, you are not alone. It is only as we withdraw and allow you to seem to stand on your own alone that you learn and grow. And it is our growth and our victory, too. We are eternally grateful to you for this.

I leave you with the thought that as we go forward together, there will be a greater closeness—but ironically, a greater objectivity—in your writings. Some day I may entrance you to bring through pure thinking unaffected by your presence. That does not mean to imply you are a block, but is rather a statement of further advanced work culminating in greater clarity and purity in the receiving.

I remain at your side.

Saint Germain

5:37 A.M.
January 16, 1988
West Grove, Pennsylvania

CHAPTER TWENTY-TWO

FULFILLING YOUR HEAVENLY DESTINY EVERY DAY

Greetings, Philip, on this holy morning. It is good to come to you. It was decided that I, T. P.[4], should come to you first today. This is a first, isn't it? We wanted to lead you in higher understanding. You can feel my warmth, can't you? Yes, you can.

It Is Grace to See Ourselves as God Sees Us

Philip, I want to talk about your (our) work. You have been impressed with a broad vision. You *can* trust the sequence of events that have come to your life. You cannot always see or understand the correlation or compatibility between our guidance and your earthly circumstances. From our vantage point we can see far in advance the unfolding events in your life. What we say to you in the moment may seem meaningless or irrelevant, in light of your present earthly reality. But as time passes you start to see the value, purpose, love, and wisdom behind our guidance; your life's conditions begin to show forth the reality of what we spoke many months or years prior.

---

[4]T. P.: The initials of this spirit guide have been used to maintain confidentiality. T.P. is a real person who passed into the spirit world in 1982. I had met him only once briefly during his life on earth. He has come to me more than once through several mediums since then. He was known and loved by many on earth for his unstoppable zeal and love for God. He continues in this same aura of energy in spirit.

The appearances of things on earth are not equal to happenings in spirit. There are yet many mysteries for you on earth. Imagine tearing away all darkness, all ignorance, all blindness on earth and opening earth's people to the light of God. How dark earth would seem by comparison. How easily and suddenly the hearts of men would be known. Stripped of all pretense, all sham, we would know others and ourselves as we truly are. This revelation would shock people into change.

We are barred from revealing this reality to most, and even when allowed, we may do it only in the spirit of love, not condemnation. And then only gradually. This revelation is often seen at a moment of apparent death as in accidents. In that apparently fatal moment, the real life, the heart, the thinking, and all the deeds of life flash in panoramic view before our eyes. We know ourselves as we are known. Such experiences are grace, for hopefully we see and we change from our own self-made destruction. Lucky, ultimately, is the person who sees himself in this way. With the masses of humanity, such revealing comes slowly; ever so thoughtfully do we let the inner self be known to each one. It is frightening to see this real self at times. But we reveal the holy aspects too, to encourage, but mostly to reveal the full range of truth pertaining to any one soul.

Knowledge Available in the Spirit World Is Limitless

We take this time to explain by the above analogy that there is much that your earthly existence, your earth knowledge and understanding, does not show in ultimate reality. In fact, it covers up that reality at times. There is a vast amount of information about many areas of life after death which are unknown to your side. There is no mundane information here. All is vital. We see things as they are. Here life originated, so all the science is here to explain its beginnings if we merit such knowledge and desire to know.

Just the field of light and color could take eternity to study and comprehend. We need not know all that is to be known on this topic to see and experience light and color in our world, but such knowledge is available.

Then there is the world or study of history. Everything is recorded here, including precise, individual records as well as the records of masses of people and civilizations. Even though in earth time we don't need so long to read and grasp the truth, it would still take eternity to grasp just this one subject: the cultures and history of the human race.

On and on we could go to make our point. We realize, we see fully, the confusion that comes between what you know and what we share and are able to share. Did you know that instead of this slow, slow—and, what is to us, primitive—way of receiving in writing, we could in one single vision give you infinite information that is so complete, so comprehensive, so detailed as to contain a complete message, a complete understanding? We need only flash upon your consciousness this picture. Were you ready and able to receive it, we could easily communicate much information in a single picture or series of pictures. Do we not do this already in the dream state? Yes, we do, and this is a gift to so receive and understand. All humans have this capacity.

Spirit Guides Are Still Perfecting Their Own Growth

Back to the original point: Do not be dismayed if all that comes to you is not to your liking or entirely correct according to your present understanding. Sometimes we mean well from this side, but we too are capable of falling short of perfection, not because perfection is impossible, but because we too are still growing and learning. Mankind is evolving together in this area. God works through man to man and these relationships, at best, leave improvement to be desired. But we do the best we can.

You will be challenged indeed to understand, to translate our transmissions into earthly explanations. Fortunately we have eternity to make all things straight. This is also unfortunate, because so long as we can't fully understand each other, neither can we achieve perfect oneness, perfect harmony. Having a personal indwelling of God makes up the difference. At the very least, through Him we can maintain patience and understanding and *love*.

I simply wanted to touch in here to calm your concerns. Keep on doing as you are and look most positively upon all of this. We know of your concern for truth. It is ours, too. But be patient to see the grand scheme of things uncovered, so that you can see your part in the overall plan. This is more than important—it is vital! We place our hope in you and so far do not feel it is misplaced. Things will become clearer and clearer. Always remember that you are a channel. You hold within you the capacity to limit or expand the degree of use. We, especially I, understand well your ardent desire for the highest truth to come through you always. Keep this desire alive, it is not in vain; such expectancy will draw the highest to you.

Remember that this is a "growing and groaning" relationship. Growing, because you and we are learning, and painful because we must strip away all ignorance and falsehood. I, myself, did not come over here entirely enlightened. I needed a whole life to know all that I could have known had I stayed on earth longer. At the very least I came here with dedication and zeal above average. My love was willing, but not perfected. I awakened into a world of surprises when I passed over to this plane. Oh, what surprises! For all the world-bound explanations could never give a tiny fraction of what lies ahead!

It Is Essential to Control and Direct Your Thoughts

I can say that the most essential aspect of life on earth is to control and direct thought. Master thought, and essentially you will be at home here. Out of mastery of thought comes the mastery of love. Think on this, for it is given with deeper purpose than merely to speak philosophically. Keep on keeping on. Know that in essence you have discerned and followed correctly. The external issues are not important. Love and truth rule here. Check yourself in this department first and foremost.

As I started to say above, what we communicate down the road will be different from what we communicate today. Familiarity with each other guarantees clearer and clearer communication. So, as you are keeping on, so are we too. Be an open, loving vessel and you cannot, will not, fail! You must know that! I pass on the baton to beloved Saint Germain and bid you farewell in word, but in reality I am never away. You and all those like you are in my heart.

J. P.

Saint Germain:

It is glorious to rise with the new day on earth. This is Saint Germain. Earth, even in its less than perfect state, is the womb of mankind and therefore is central to our thoughts. It is most central to Him, in whose spirit we come.

Life on Earth Is Vital Preparation for Eternal Existence

There is so much beauty on earth. The intrinsic beauty of symbiotic relationships in nature is in itself so meaningful to observe. The Creator's thought, heart, and will manifested in and on planet Earth is a joy to behold. You have the saying, "Trite, but true." There is *nothing* trite about God's purpose on earth and man's existence here. You want for other worlds, other experiences on earth when you have yet to grasp the most elementary of principles of life that cry out for your recognition and service on earth. You cease to grasp the true purpose and true understanding of how very essential your earthly life is to your eternal existence. So you cannot appreciate the greatness, the importance of this phase, this very short phase, of your life.

Do not long to come here or to grasp all that lies ahead of you in spirit, earthlings. Seek most to understand life there on earth. Know its essential, paramount, vital, primary relationship to what your nature will be here, upon the day of your arrival.

Your masses follow mass whims, mass fashions, mass thinking. And then, because the masses go this way, you call it reality. The masses are far from knowing true life and the purpose of life on earth. Do not follow mass instinct, for nine times out of ten, it is wrong. Be different in knowing and living for truth and the highest of highest loves. Be aware that at this moment, wherever you are, earthlings, you are on your way to your eternal destiny. But you paint the canvas of that future life now with every stroke of your life's emanations on earth. You are determining your own destiny. The picture you now paint will be hanging in God's great abode for you to see the moment you expire, and part with your earthly body.

You Are the Master Artist of Self. Paint a Divine Canvas!

Go to a museum and observe the masters. Find the perfection in every stroke thoughtfully placed on the canvas. Observe, too, the imperfections. Both are there. It cannot be different, for cause and effect are as operative in our world as the sun's rising and setting in yours. Be master artists in your life. There is still time to scrape flaws off the canvas of your life so you can paint over in perfect strokes the unfolding subject matter.

Be masters of yourselves now, and arrive here to glimpse that perfection in all that awaits you, to reflect that earthly journey you presently call life. It is life only if it is of God, if it contains God. This above all is the prerequisite of self-mastery. If He is at the center of all that you do on earth, then your eternal life's portrait in spirit realms will be a canvas with love as its theme, and its full expression. And such a picture can only be made up of—filled with—all light.

Do not labor in vain when you labor. Labor with a heart of love and all will be glorious when you arrive to join us in this world of the new expression of your life. All that you are and all that you are doing can end only in the climax of a second birth into this world. Pauper and prince alike, our destiny is the same. None can avoid the transition from that plane to this, none. There are *no* exceptions to this reality. Take your stand now. Be all serious with this decision, for it is *the* most important decision you have to make.

Awaken to the Responsibility for Your Soul's Growth

Eternity is not something we choose, it is something that is. And we are a part of eternity. So your ultimate choice is not to decide if you accept eternity or not, but whether you shall accept full and complete responsibility for the *results* manifested here after you pass on to us. Do not falter in this responsibility.

Once this reality dawns in the human mind, God has won in His purpose and the revolution of soul begins. Repentance naturally follows, and change of conduct follows repentance very closely. Reformation of the human condition begins with this revelation as spoken above.

I give this message to awakening humanity. I give it with love and compassion—not pity. Awaken to reality! Awaken to responsibility! Awaken to responsibility assumed by taking up self-mastery in love!

This is my message today through this instrument. It is not his message alone. He did not come by it by forethought, but by the force of my urgent cry to awaken humanity. Now is the time to choose your eternal destiny! With all the love of God that my small soul can contain, I appeal to you, I come to you! Awake and rise, fulfill your heavenly destiny!

In the spirit of Christ,
Saint Germain

5:46 A.M.
January 31, 1988
West Grove, Pennsylvania

CHAPTER TWENTY-THREE

STAY THE COURSE WITH GOD

Our sentiments were in your prayer this morning. You need such determination to win the final battle of self. Everyone is looking to win over forces at large. But it is the change of each soul, one by one, that reverses the destructive course of history. If only each of us could realize our value in this way: "I must change, for I am part of the whole and as I and others change then the whole is changed." Our individual existence makes up the whole. Without the individual there is no whole. Therefore, never take yourself or any other human for granted. There is no such thing as unimportant, unneeded. All are needed. It is vital and important for each to change concretely so that the abstract whole can change.

We Help to Raise and to Transform Your Energies

The Father Himself sees the individual, not the whole, at a distance. The unity of individuals appears as a special beauty for God to behold. Still, it is the unity *within* the individual that makes it possible for individuals to be united as a whole. Beauty of a united person is first and most important and unity among individuals is secondary and resultant. Therefore, the individual is most precious to God.

What you are now experiencing is the same as my embodiment in you recently. Special energies are drawn about you for this purpose. The consistency of your efforts has made this more and more possible. You have done your part, we have done ours. This will continue at a steady and expanded rate. You are reaching for levels necessary to do your mission. As you reach these inner levels of development, we will respond, helping you to greater and greater awareness and to the fulfillment of your life's purpose.

As you have experienced, we do work on your energies. We must enter into your vibration, your holy and sacred self. To do this, a foundation of rapport and trust must be built between us. You worry of failures and downfalls. We look past these to potential. We must or our energies will stagnate at negative and lesser levels. Ours is the specific mission of helping you to raise your focus of thought to success and to embrace positive ideas. Only in this way do we truly elevate your energies. Your predominant thought becomes chief among your many thoughts and compels you unwittingly to dwell where that prevailing thought lies. We work to dominate you with love and service and loving thoughts—positive, uplifting thoughts. And as you see the result of these thoughts in your life and life's energies, you will gravitate more and more toward consistency in thinking and living positively. What else is becoming, or transformation?

We Never Violate Your Freedom

We come to overshadow you first with thoughts and feelings of love—to penetrate your soul and to imbue you with divine energy. We come to fill your being with the very perfume of heavenly delight. We come to raise and transform your internal existence. And in a moment of life's retrospective thinking, you can see we have been increasingly successful. Are you not more and more positive? Are you not more and more free? Truly free! Are you not more and more filled with thoughts and feelings of hope? Is this not a part of our influence over time through mutual effort and cooperation?

We stand waiting each week to meet you in the temple of your mind. We impart consistent thoughts which have raised your thinking, expanded your awareness. At any one moment, we have the knowledge and the power to expand your awareness greatly in any direction desired. Even evil forces have this capacity and often exert it when the instrument allows it. But, ours is a path of patience strictly in accordance with divine love and divine law. We would no more violate your inner freedoms to do and to be than we would want ours to be violated. This makes our work painful at times as you know, but by law and love it cannot be otherwise.

So, step by step you have been raised. And the influence you have had on others' lives is not insignificant. Step by step you have been raising others, consciously and unconsciously, to higher levels of life. And through this we have been able to enter more completely into their lives. This is heaven's purpose and heaven's way.

More is yet to come. Know beyond doubt this one thing: Every step on the path to the fulfillment of this work is laid out. As you need and are ready to receive, the way will be clearly shown. The right people and places will be made available to you (and, we must add) far above the usual. To you there will be apparent and unarguable signs that this is so and this will ease your flow into the next step. But always pray and meditate to stay on course.

Follow Your Heart to Find Your Destiny

The accumulated efforts of your heart's longing and your life's pursuits have made today's work possible. You must know that you did not suddenly bump into this mission as one bumps into an object in the darkness of night. No! You have been on this course and passed through specific suffering, and some even at your own hands, to come to this day. You must not believe otherwise. This has been your destiny since birth. And in this destiny there was needed certain inner conditions of heart, especially. And these conditions included most specifically a sensitivity to higher vibrations, creating awareness beyond average. How else do you think we could have touched in with you, captured your attention and held it?

When a man truly meets his life's destiny he knows. And he becomes completely absorbed in it, even to the point of losing sleep and sensation of hunger. Such is your life and the unfolding of your existence. Your life is a mathematical equation.

Life experience plus inclination plus inner design (by God's volition) equals mission. All the ingredients in your life, mixed together and cooked over the flame of God's love, have brought forth the results that now appear so obviously in your being. It could not have been otherwise. Know this!

God Intercedes to Guarantee Your Success

If you had not been so you would have perished long ago. But more than anything God needs champions who win exceedingly over this world. Such are the people He can use to save this world. Such souls are indeed grateful and most useful for His purposes. Saint Paul appeared before you in prayer today for this was his plight and you identified with him from youth and were impressed to do so from youth because of your destiny. From these higher altitudes of life we can see many decades ahead to the destiny of individuals' lives. And it is our mission when assigned to an individual to lead them on this course.

You often wonder and then reflect in realization upon the answer to your wonderment thus: Why me, I have made so many mistakes and still blunder from time to time? But, Philip, what you *do not* see is the road *beyond* the bend. We do, and we know what is around it. We see what you suffer far in advance of its actual happening. But we also see the outcome. Depending on the ancestral and individual merit there are certain times when choices eliminate our direct influence and persons choose the wrong path. We, knowing still the unequivocal destiny of such individuals, work after the fact of wrongful choice to lead them back to the path. The degree to which he or she is pure in heart coupled with the degree to which his or her ancestors have been of the same heart will determine the degree of predestination. When one has such potential and is thus chosen of God, God Himself places an energy, a force about that person not to protect him from suffering, but to *guarantee* his overcoming and eventual, complete success.

If God did not intercede in this way there would not be hope for mankind at all. The Christ is such a man. In the midst of unbelievable suffering God brought glory to his life and eventual success. Evil stood *haughtily* in the way and God had to let Jesus pass through the fires and tortures of hell. Still, in spite of his suffering, Jesus never gave up or abandoned his mission. His heart never changed. In such people God can entrust and invest everything.

Stay the course as you are, and your end will be successful. The heart is the temple of God in man. And in the final count it is here that we win or lose. A man with a strong love for God will never die, nor can his love be truly extinguished. Such a person is a winner in the end regardless of the outward view.

5:40 A.M.
April 17, 1988
West Grove, Pennsylvania

Your security lies in God, not in man or material things. Only God is perfect. And man is made perfect only to the degree that he allows God to manifest in him. Man's ego must get out of the way. Man must relieve himself of self-awareness to reach awareness through God. Only by staying close to Him is this possible.

Have a Steady Heart—Love Friend and Foe Alike

Man is unpredictable and therefore very predictable. Unless you make allowance for this you will ride a roller coaster of life. Return quickly always to the only stable center in life. Realign yourself with Him and ask Him for His heart in you. It is easier on paper than in practice. It is not just a philosophy of life but a reality to be obtained.

You will not be destroyed by one incident in life. We love you under all circumstances and do not change our support and protection when the winds blow ill across your life. We are from Him who is unchanging in His commitment to bring you home.

And though He may allow you to learn through suffering or He Himself may chastise you, it is always from love that He does so. There is never a time when this central energy is not loving.

You see from your recent conflict with another person that if you allow your spirit to enter into anything less than love, you disturb your own balance. God cannot disturb His balance, for He would destroy not only Himself but all life as well. While He hurts, He cannot afford to lose control. It is not in His nature to let go, to be less than He is. There is a higher and greater lesson to learn tonight as you ponder your pain. As long as you are steady, as long as you give His love to friend and foe alike, your work will be successful. He is the center of your work and it is He to whom you are bringing others. We work to bridge each person's transition from where they are to oneness with God. But we serve His cause, only!

Lead Others by Love, Not Fear

Fear nothing as long as you keep your course. Nothing—no one—can replace you; nor can anyone rob you. Be steady in Him and give all glory to Him. You cannot worry about another, nor can you stop them. Let *us* take authority over him or her. You must merely pray for them to release the energies for us to help. We cannot trick others into faith or spirituality. We cannot convince them by pushing or demanding. Do your best before God. Perform always your duties before Him. Do not stand aloof of others but lead them with the truth as revealed by us. And remember that the highest love is to give the highest truth either in word or in action. I have told you that we can help you only when you are yourself. This is true of all.

Do as you have been learning. Empathize with others—put yourself in their place—and love them as yourself. Treat them as if they were you. Treat them as deserving and they will become so.

Use all circumstances to master self for release from self. Do not be ashamed to admit wrong, for in so doing others can and will and you will be freed also. Use this as a stepping stone to a higher level. You are elder; raise the relationship to deeper and higher understanding. Remember always that everyone will follow out of love, whereas only a few follow out of fear.

You know the forces that help you and surround you. Trust them. When you rise, many rise. Doors are opening—do not be afraid at all!!!

Keep the course and all will be well. We surround you as one body to defend the truth and love of God.

Saint Germain

9:15 P.M.
April 18, 1988
West Grove, Pennsylvania

CHAPTER TWENTY-FOUR

JESUS AND THE PRINCIPLE OF TRANSFORMATION

This is Saint Germain. Greetings this morning. I will be with you for the duration of this writing, but Saint Paul will speak also. There is a need to touch in for—as I told you while you awakened—your energies are weakening and you need this contact. As I spoke to you yesterday, your writings are a form of prayer to you. Without going inward to the mind, you cannot maintain the inner contact with us through which you receive the energies necessary for your work.

Every Mission Bears Its Own Price Tag

We know you have many questions. And we know that you are dissatisfied on many levels of your work. Nevertheless, we want your continued determination and patience. You often think in former terms of getting ahead—of working hard—of completing the work. And we have cautioned you that these applied only to your past work. Because of the fine attunement necessary for your mediumship, you must work somewhat—though not completely—differently. You will complete your mission by working most fully upon mediumship. And this is not something that can be rushed nor achieved by simply working harder in the outer work. The attunement to us is most vital.

We know you are lonely. It is a lonely work that you do. Sitting for hours each week to meditate and pray is very much alone from earth's perspective. But not from ours.

You may drop your mediumship any day, but you will see how uncomfortable you will feel in so doing. This is because your natural design, your natural ability and inclination, is for this work. Again, you concern yourself with paying a price, a karmic price. Yes, you do, and yes, you will. All missions have a price tag on them. It is the nature of life in the conditions of the world today. It is a question of wisdom in the application of your life's energies. Pick and choose wisely how and for whom you use your energies.

Master the Correct Use of Your Time and Energy

Along this line, we are happy that you assert yourself in what you must do. To those who scatter their energies, you will appear selfish. But, we say that mediums especially draw to themselves people from all walks of life and at every level of society. Unless you are master over your energies, someone else either on earth or in spirit will be.

We have never demanded that you do this or that because we know it is against the principle of free will to demand. Rather, we respect your energies and act accordingly. Not everyone—incarnate or discarnate—will do so.

What you are doing is a great responsibility. Therefore, take command always regarding your use of time. This gives you dignity and authority which will draw to you in spirit those who are like you. People take advantage of kindness if it is unprotected by wisdom. Because you speak not from self but represent heaven's view, then you must—without being overbearing—maintain objectivity and control of your energies.

Suffering, to Have Value, Must Be Transformed

As we continue, I want to speak on your sleepless, restless, cold night. The solution was simple—close the windows. But you said upon awakening that you didn't have the "presence of mind." That is true. It is a good object lesson for taking all experiences positively. We see that you have done that. Thinking of those who suffer around the world due to weather or lack of necessities is to lift your own suffering to a universal level. At this level, your suffering can be transformed into light. This is alchemy at its highest.

Suffering for suffering's sake is valueless. Unfortunately, most of humanity has and will continue to do so. Much time must pass for the masses to awaken, though we work on it night and day. Only when we transform all our energies to positive ends, can we rise from where we are to a higher level. This includes everything. It applies even to the most bitter and painful of suffering. Jesus told us to pray for our enemies. And who are our enemies but those who hurt us in some way? Prayer transforms this suffering energy to constructive ends and elevates us. Enter into negative, self-pitying energies and you stagnate and remain at the same level or, if continued, you will go down.

Even now, as you write, you are gravitating toward negativity about "feeling" little as you write. You could move into energies that turn you away from us. By working through and beyond personal feelings, beyond self-concern, and by dwelling upon your guidance, you are transforming your energies. It is difficult for man on earth to grasp the reality and power of thought. As you lift your thoughts by their very content or subject matter, you also lift your entire spirit. "Where your thoughts are, there your real you is, also." So it always stands as a central guiding principle that you must focus your mind-energy—thoughts—upon subject matter that is positive. Then, whatever the circumstances, you can be successful.

Meditation Is a Valuable Tool for Transformation

True meditation involves this very dynamic of raising thought, focusing thought, directing thought. As you do so, you go into a finer vibration. You go into a frequency that is more spiritual and easier for us to come in on. Most people struggle in meditation because they get caught up in the mechanics of it. Mechanics are a means unto the end of raising the thought by which you raise not only thought, but also your spirit being.

The purity of any spiritual experience is directly proportionate to the degree to which thought is raised. Fundamentally what determines the degree of raising thought is its subject matter.

When you begin your writings or readings you have experienced frustration at tuning in. As in this morning's writing, you had an aversion to going on. However, you now see that as the subject of your writings changed and moved to more objective, universal concerns, your feelings overall changed. This follows the principle of which I speak. Always, the secret of raising energies is to examine the content of your thought. The content not only provides the basis for give and take, it also determines with whom you converse.

Many are suffering in life because they are the focus of their thoughts and never transform life's precious energies to a higher purpose. Self remains the center of their thought life. There is no transformation in such thoughts. If you must be concerned with self, direct such thoughts to God and make Him leader of yourself, thus raising your mind's content from self to the highest Being in the cosmos. This is an empirical reality as seen from this side.

Jesus: a Supreme Example of Self-Transformation

Jesus was unique in history because he learned the art and principle of self-transformation quite early in life. He did not feel self-pity, but empathy for God and others. He learned how to take the negative and make it positive. His whole life course was so guided. By the time he reached the cross, he knew how to raise his thoughts to victory, to be triumphant over the evil that sought to destroy him.

But who before Jesus and before Abraham and before the beginning of time as you know it learned to use mental discipline to transform, to utilize energy? It was God the Father. He taught Jesus personally and with the help of great souls in spirit, and through angels also.

This capacity to transform energy is the quality of the Christ within each of us. Christ is but an earthly title to define a prototype—a working model of a man who demonstrated transformation on the cross. It is not his crucifixion that makes him unique. It is his transforming possible defeat into victory, keeping his energies focused and raised to God. This is his uniqueness and this is God's way.

You use the word "restoration" when referring to this process. It is the same meaning, for nothing can simply be changed from one state to another with no passage of time on your earth plane. To take something from a lesser level to a greater and higher level is to restore it to its original ideal state. This also is transformation. At this moment you are transforming your mind energy to an elevated level near God. This is where you were when you were born, without negative thought, totally innocent of negative thinking. You are bringing your mind back to this original, innocent state.

Jesus said that the Kingdom could not be entered into unless one became like a little child. This is so and it means totally accepting, seeing all people in a positive light and as worthy of our love.

So, Philip, take this writing into consideration when you go about your day. Traditionally, religious people begin their day in prayer. The real reason for this is to make the Father the center of your thought. With Him as your center, you can't go wrong. Through this process, neutral to negative energies stagnating around and in you can be changed and transformed! Unless we are seriously going about our daily tasks with this idea in mind, we may simply be going through the motions without being transformed, as our life unfolds.

Successful people are those who, through mental discipline (self-mastery), habitually transform all of their life energies—good and bad—into victory. All humanity must ultimately gain such self-mastery, applying it moment by moment to achieve victory over the lower self by the higher self. Man must eradicate wrong-doing and evil in the world by starting with himself through self-mastery and self-transformation. You know already of what I speak.

Now, rest and refresh and return as Saint Paul stands by waiting to speak to you.

Saint Germain

This is Saint Paul. I have come to you because I too am one who touches in with you and have done so from time to time. It was through your former teacher, Dr. Kim[5], that my relationship with you was heightened.

As you saw me walk toward you this morning, it was a foretoken of my coming directly into your life, and I shall continue to do so from time to time. There is a great necessity for all of this as we both know.

Study the Lives of Saints and Martyrs

I want to encourage you, my son, with your work, for it is beyond you or your ability to hold back the flood tide of the Father's desire. Unless we take these actions and plunge through to the depth of humanity's needs by this intercessory, spiritual activity, the whole will not be fulfilled.

Return to my writings in the New Testament to touch in with my energies, for there is an intention here to educate you, to prepare you. When you were in Korea[6], I walked ever so closely with you. It was Saint Anthony[7], first—and I later—who prepared you in your walk until the baton for spiritual alchemy was handed over to Brother Germain. He now guides you and those around you most closely.

When you walked alone in Korea, you read my writings and wept. I too wept when I wrote that essay on love, for I too was lacking in God's love. I was not perfect and needed transformation through Jesus' influence upon my heart.

---

[5] Dr. Kim is one of my former spiritual teachers who had a Ph.D. in Christian Theology and knew her spirit guide to be Saint Paul. She was on earth at the time of this receiving from Saint Paul but passed into the spirit world in 1989.

[6] I served in the U.S. Army at Camp Casey bordering Tong Du Chon, Korea, just 15 miles below the 38th parallel from June 1962 to June 1963.

[7] Saint Anthony, a 15th-century German monk, began appearing at my bedside when I was a small child. My mother told me that I used to tell her about "a man who had been standing by my bed" at times when she would come into my room in the morning to wake me up.

The writings of your contemporary Bible cannot begin to contain the reality of my life's activities. Many times I was in despondency—alone like a man in a desert on a dark night. Experience upon experience—trial and error if you will—taught me that only by transforming my situation to constructive ends could I open the portals of heaven even as the door to my Roman prison was opened by spirit. By that time, I knew completely the art of transformation! You stood there[8] yourself because you were being prepared. And so I too am with you today to speak of transformation.

We know every tear you have shed. And we know how you have suffered trying to rid yourself of self. Through the guidance of spirit and of those who truly have loved you on earth, you are being gradually transformed. This is a part of the larger plan.

Remember me always as I, Saint Paul, have been one of those in spirit who has brought you closer to your real self. I am always available to you and I shall make myself known through others. Believe with all your heart that you are guided minute by minute.

To the glory of God and in the love of Christ, I remain near you for the cause of world freedom!

Saint Paul

6:27 A.M.
June 28, 1988
West Grove, Pennsylvania

---

[8] While on business in Rome in 1982, I visited the Forum where my tour guide took me to see the prison cell in which Saint Paul had been held. I actually stood inside the cell. It was a very moving experience.

CHAPTER TWENTY-FIVE

PURIFY YOUR ENERGY THROUGH THE GOD WITHIN

Not everything, not every thought comes from spirit. You have your own thoughts. However, every soul is moving upward toward his highest self. To so move, he is assisted at every level. And those who are with him are like him in some ways, in basic ways, or they could not establish an identity with him nor rapport. To serve such a soul, which means every soul, is the responsibility of us in spirit. When our debts of service for wrongs done while on earth are paid, we may continue to serve because that is our inclination.

The New Age Is the Christ Age

Today a new age is dawning. Many call it the Christ Age. But few realize just how much of the Christ Age it truly is! The Second Coming is at hand, and this and this alone makes this age the New Age. Otherwise, what is truly new? It is the Christ Age also because when He comes He comes to lead all men and women, both on earth and in spirit, to their highest self—the Christ self. Yesterday, we said that Christ is the one who was able to achieve complete transformation—turning all obstacles to his advantage, and using them to dominate and destroy evil's effect on him. The crucifixion is an example of such transformation. Fixing his heart upon the Father, Jesus transformed defeat into victory, darkness into light. To Jesus, nothing was so real as his Heavenly Father and His will.

I wanted to emphasize transformation again today because that is our task when serving you or any other soul on earth. We seek to have you see reality from God's point of view, that in seeing you may be transfixed and transformed! We are about the work of transformation hourly.

By Serving Others We Parent Them

To support others and help them continue from day to day is to encourage them, to speak of positive possibilities, to point out the path to victory. We must consistently point the way to a positive outcome; we must constantly remind the soul in our care to have faith, to keep going.

In a world so fraught with obstacles it is difficult for all of you to keep going, to be always positive, to have unwavering faith. And yet, you must. Otherwise, into what state will your mind fall? Where will you find yourselves on the morrow? It is foolish and a needless waste of time to look back, to repeat mistakes, or to digress in any way!

This is our work. And in serving, we actually parent. We are teacher, doctor, father and mother, friend all rolled into one. Those who are parents understand that parenting is a constant job. And when you love, especially, you do not mind. It is often a heart-rending burden, but nevertheless a happy burden. When children leave the nest and the door closes on the last one, there is pain in the heart of the parents. Their burdens may be gone as they have known them, but they will feel lost unless they find new ones to serve—to parent.

Such is our task. We want to remove from the mind the

thought that there is something strange or mystical about our presence and assistance. In true love it is all so natural. And those who have loved another because they are they and not from duty will readily understand our state of mind, our state of heart.

The More We Serve, the More We Love

You see, dear ones, before we loved those whom we serve, God, our Father, loved them. And being all-knowing as He is, He knows each one of us as an ideal in His mind. Because you are literally His offspring, there is no burden too heavy for Him to bear in helping you. Such is the nature of a parent's heart. Such is our heart, who come on His behalf.

The more we serve you, the more we love you. To the point that while there are times you do not need us directly by your side, you are never out of our thoughts. And even if we are off assisting another or at some needful task in the world we dwell in, we return quickly when you are in dire need.

Is this so different from your world? Doesn't a mother or father of five, eight, or ten children know them each by name? And are these beloved offspring ever truly out of mind? No, they are not. And do you not also rush to their side, even after they are grown, and help them in dire need? Yes, you do. So, what is so different?

The difference lies in time. Because we dwell in thought itself we can come and go faster than you. Many of you on earth stay in contact with your children by so-called intuition or ESP. Is this means of staying in contact not the same as our remaining mindful of those whom we serve though we are at a distance? They are one and the same. It is a matter of degree. Those who regularly practice tuning in and have loved sacrificially will grow in this ability and always know the conditions surrounding those whom they have loved.

You Are Part of the Evolution of Consciousness

In this age now dawning, humanity is awakening more and more to the creative, practical use of intuition. It will take time for all to come to the same level. But, it is coming. One thousand years from now, we will see an entirely new humanity upon the earth. Just as the world of one thousand years ago is different from today, so will the world be different one thousand years from now.

You are all a part of the evolution in consciousness. You cannot escape it. And if you could be one with the very Force bringing the New Age into existence, you would not want to escape. See your struggles and overcoming as part of the whole— do not see them isolated and develop self-pity or bitterness. Embrace all that happens to you and see it as a part of the whole of mankind. As you mark history, there have been many ages. But for the Father there is a gradual progression from a world of ignorance and darkness to an age and world of total understanding and total light. Each successive step for Him has been toward the fulfillment of that one goal on earth! Therefore, neither He nor we have rested, because we see and experience the continuum, with its full force from this side.

Why would we continue except that we too are a part of the whole? From our side it is so obvious! And we can clearly see that unless you dear ones are completely one with Him, we cannot be happy. For your unhappiness, your suffering—by its association with the very streams of energy passing throughout creation, including man—is our unhappiness also.

Not everyone in spirit can see this. Only those who are sufficiently elevated to see the whole can see all the inner relationships among mankind. You may not be my brother or sister by earthly birth, but you are made so through the love of the

Father and Parent God who is the Parent of us all, not figuratively, but literally! Literally! Literally!

To Achieve Self-Realization, Practice What You Teach

We come to earth this day to add to the discourse we have started and to expand through it your understanding. As you come to know you will be awakened progressively to ultimate reality. Then He and we can come closer and closer to revealing our complete selves to you. This is our ultimate purpose and goal. We have said again and again that you must realize God is within and without. As you increasingly discover this reality you shall appreciate, out of your own heart, the truths of which we speak.

There is still another point to be made in our message today: Whatever is your preoccupation is also you. Where your thoughts and your love dwell most—that is where you are. Even though we speak through this instrument, if he himself does not follow the value, the lessons, in these messages, but instead focuses upon pride in himself and his mediumship, his heart will be upon self and not upon God's and mankind's needs. Consequently, he will not learn and grow and become the individual needed by us for eternal, higher purposes. He is not exempt from growth and the need to learn. Let his heart be upon the lessons contained in his own writings.

At times, when he has not absorbed the lesson imparted in a previous message we do not pass on more until he does. And yet, we do not speak to him alone. In the beginning, yes. But not now. Now what comes to him is both personal and universal in nature.

Our point is this: First, your thoughts are vibratory and make up the energy that surrounds you. Thus, you carry the atmosphere of who and what you are at all times. A sensitive can easily discern this fact and its manifestation. This energy that surrounds you also contains thoughts which we have imparted to you that remain with you. In this sense also our influence never leaves you. The more each one dwells upon these leading, uplifting thoughts, the more the energy around him multiplies into goodness. Mantras, prayers, chants, spiritual reading (the Bible, for instance), all compose the energy surrounding you. Gradually, little by little, this energy becomes purified and holy. This is our goal. But the secret lies in the transformation of our individual thought life. This is transformed by consistently turning and turning again and again to heaven. By displacement and replacement, new, higher energies are derived.

You Are Never Unattended on Your Path toward God

Many of us have habitually and repeatedly thought and spoken negatively. We created an energy around us that comes to multiply and convolute. We become trapped in the web of our own thoughts. We lose freedom of will and our own destructive, bad habits come to dominate us.

Then it is with great effort that we have to begin our journey out of negative thoughts. Often the novice beginning the path of soul evolution is easily discouraged. So enormous does the obstacle of self in his thought life seem to be that he easily gives up. But face it he must, even crawling in humility upon his knees to grope and climb his way out. His thoughts have become like a choking jungle of undergrowth and vines, so dense as to cut out almost all light. Like a man with a machete he must hack away with new thoughts. To do so he must think about his goal—that pinpoint of light and love ahead in the far distance.

Wherever the soul may be in its journey away from ego, away from self—away from evil, if you will—we are there. The pilgrim is never unattended and he is ever facing himself to see what he must change. We do not abandon him because he seems unpleasant to work with. For in him we see our past selves. Or by helping our earthly counterpart when we too are not yet free, we wage redemptive war against our past.

We are truly one. And we want you to see this above all: Wherever you are on the journey to yourself, totally in God, you are never, never alone!

In conclusion, you can see your thoughts are yours to do with as you will. We cannot force you to think in such and such a way. We can only patiently guide you—even if it takes a lifetime. You must realize that you are never alone in your efforts to rise and stand tall for eternity. We are all one family in Him and as Christ returns, as surely He must, we will complete our journey from His road map as we not only conclude the New Age but become the living reality in spirit and on earth of all God's dreams for us.

God bless the reader in his journey home.

Saint Germain

10:40 A.M.
June 30, 1988
West Grove, Pennsylvania

Part Six
Love: Divine and Human

CHAPTER TWENTY-SIX

VALENTINE'S DAY MESSAGE ON LOVE

All that you have just thought and prayed, I too have heard and felt. My heart longs to bring to earth the wisdom of the ages. But you on earth expect our expression to be cloaked in adroit, specially phrased words. Intellectualism loves glorious, long words. A sign of higher learning on earth is the use of abstract words understood by a select few within a particular field. But this is not necessarily truth from a high level. Great souls strip language of its pretense and present the essence of truth in an economy of words. Truth is simple. And it is the combination of simple words, each understood universally, that most clearly conveys pure truth.

Love and Truth Are Simple and Universal

If we take just the word "love," as you celebrate its existence on this earthly February fourteenth day—it is but a single word of four letters. Though simple in its outer, literal expression, it carries a universal message, a universal truth understood by all. Just plain "LOVE." Why must we wrap it in complicated coverings. Love, the act of caring, serving another as we want and need to be cared for, and served. So simple, so supreme in the English language, or any other language.

The most erudite person is fascinated by this word, love. It conjures up in each of us warm feelings, longing feelings. It expresses our essence: to be, and to help others to be. L-O-V-E. Who needs a college education to understand love? Even those who can neither read nor write can understand love.

Pure truth is simple because we know its definition, its meaning, its expression by the essence of our being. Truth is because God is, and because all that He created, is. This is the beginning of knowledge, the beginning of wisdom. It could be no simpler than that.

And so, as we pour out information from above, we could carry on the pretense that the more obscure the meaning of something, the higher, the more elevated it is. But this is simply not so. How much simpler can you get, than to say all things are composed of energy and energy is atoms in flux, set in a certain relationship? And that each atom is made up of a nucleus and an electron shell. How much simpler can life be at its core? It is beautiful and yet profound in itself—in its simple, beautiful self.

Truth and true love often elude modern man because he fails to simplify. We complicate life by over-examination and over-explanation. This spoils our perception and puffs us up with knowledge alone. Conversely, we rise above life as we *come down* from our pretense, from our lofty, pseudo-intellectualism. These will never save us, never make us whole.

We would never diminish the importance of formal language, the language which is needed to express ideas in a precise way, either broad or specific. Man prides himself in what appears sophisticated, because it is special, and he believes that he himself and a few others alone understand it. But will this knowledge bring him to heaven—can he be saved by knowledge because it is esoteric? No, that is not the case.

We must simplify; we must be childlike, remembering that the great truths of life are simple and easy to convey—but oh, how hard sometimes to learn. Because they are simple and come in "plain" wrappings, they may not be attractive to the "sophisticated."

If I should carry on in this manner, you would write a book this morning. I have made my point. And because the theme of your prayer this morning was love—L-O-V-E—I wanted to express our thought upon it and truth—which at the highest level are one and the same.

Walk Circumspectly—Do Not Be Derailed from Your Path

You pause to ponder and to continue my train of inspiration to you. This is not entirely necessary. You will learn that everything continues to flow as thought leads to thought. You ponder what I shall impart next. There are a million themes available to us, aren't there?

I impressed you with the vision of a locomotive, a train on its tracks. Think on this. Is this not an ideal analogy in itself? But you are wondering what I shall make of it and how I will lead you on with this vision.

I wish to say this: You are the train and you are the locomotive. The track is your life. You are on the right track, you are more than on the right track, you are on *the* track for you. It is your destiny. But obstacles are placed there from time to time, and you as the engineer must keep an ever sharp lookout for them. If you cruise along at top speed, without close observation you will be derailed from your path, your track. We told you, as you will recall, to walk circumspectly. This is still our admonition. You cannot afford to be derailed.

Do not mind being misunderstood, or even talked about, in a negative way. Who hasn't experienced this from time to time? We all have, even among those whom we number as our closest friends. It is, indeed, only as we keep heaven's perspective that we *do* see correctly.

Time always shows forth the goodness or error in a decision. This is a truth of the simplest form, and is as universal as the word and practice of L- O- V- E. Time will prove you right, despite your critics. Just stay on track and don't allow *anyone* to deter you from moving forward. You may pause for station stops to rest, to refuel, to stretch, to do many things. But do not be derailed!

We are watching ahead to warn you of any dangers. You have so many souls who are on the lookout. We admonish you to pray earnestly and honestly. You will then always be in the best form to see what is ahead on your track of life. It *is* only as we walk with the Father that we can maintain alertness, keenness of mind, and inner sight. There is the emanation of truth itself from Him and there are those who embody that truth and stay close by to guide you. I am but one chosen to help you in this way.

To Attain Self-Mastery, Serve and Be Served

Life needs many helpers. None—and I want to greatly emphasize this word "none"—none of us becomes spiritually mature without the help of countless souls on earth and in spirit. One of the major lessons of self-mastery is that we need others to achieve this goal. It is only in human society that we can know and practice the art of loving and perfect this art. Without others, whom shall we love and who shall love us? Oh, how we need each other!

And does this need stop when we pass on? Absolutely not! Oh, we can be alone if we desire, but we will also be very lonely. No, life continues here as there. Only here we know by *direct* observance that we are not an island unto ourselves. This awareness, this undeniable truth, looms so clearly here.

Then why are there guides and teachers, and masters and doctors? These are just titles for various roles and positions and levels of responsibility. But in no way are these positions of distance, or elevated, separate existence where we are worshipped. These responsibilities represent levels and circumferences of love and understanding.

But above all we know we have no position unless it is a position in relation to other souls. We are a chain of servers of humanity. And we return to the earth plane knowing consciously and unconsciously that we need others for our perfection. We learn quickly that as we serve we learn, we grow, we expand—we find God, the lover and server of all, within us. We discover true life. That is so apparent here.

We do not come as metaphysicians who dole out truth and stand as greater bearers of wisdom, aloof from humanity. No, we are made more and more human—divine—as we serve. By this our divinity emerges. We *lose* ourselves in our service. We discover the true joy which comes from the loss of the memory of self as we serve. We see that this is the cure-all to all ills of the human soul and is reflected in the body. Our body is cured as well.

It is all so *simple.*

The Highest Spiritual Practice Is to Love and to Serve

We do not look upon our service to anyone as drudgery. We never tire in that way here. We consider it a great privilege to serve others on earth, especially those who are also serving others. We flock to help such people; they are the easiest to serve and are always attended by a great host of souls. Like attracts like. True humility is manifest in caring for others, including Heavenly Father, at the expense of self. Such a caring person will never, never be lost but is more and more saved.

So you see, Philip, to love the human soul and its human potential in God is the highest love, the highest service. You prayed this morning to realize this burden in your heart. If your prayer were granted you would not be able to sleep at night from worry and grief. Your eyes would not cease to run with tears and your energies would not be enough. But if you really desire this, gain it by practice. Practice first thinking individually about the people, the souls within your arena of endeavor. Think long and deeply on each one. Put yourself in their place and, in doing so, know what they need. Then serve them in this need. I told you I will be as close to you as the degree of your love for those whom you serve. This is not a mere personal promise, it is the law of attraction in love.

Do not worry so much about those of us who work with you. We appreciate your prayers and kindness always—as much as any human being—for we too are human. But love those whom you serve, and that includes your immediate family. Don't over-complicate it. Pray and you will know how to love each one. Your heart knows and will tell you.

We gather around you for the purpose of loving you as you love others and to help you do the same. We are not stratified demi-gods, but people like yourself drawn to you because we in essence think and feel as you do. This includes the negative aspects of your nature, so together you and we work out our imperfections by loving others.

Not everyone who comes our way is a lovable person. But by sacrificing yourself and loving them as yourself first, you then know how to love them. Secondly, you overcome your own problems, your own failings, in love.

We are with you 100 percent in all of your love efforts, whether it is in purely loving as God does or whether it is in trying to overcome incorrect loving. We are together to learn this lesson above all lessons. This is the essence of our work and the center of your ministry.

All that you do must have at its core the word L-O-V-E. You must meditate on this night and day, because to have L-O-V-E at the center is to have G-O-D at the center. It is He who is serving us all with the greatest humility in love. We can do no less, do not want to do any less.

This is my message for Valentine's Day 1988. Did we not come full circle? Yes, we did. And as you look back you will see the theme of love—the essence of this day and your prayer—running the length of this writing.

Our theme is our salutation and our closing. Love others as we have loved you!

Saint Germain and Band

5:40 A.M.
February 14, 1988
West Grove, Pennsylvania

CHAPTER TWENTY-SEVEN

POSITIVE KARMA AND GOD'S LOVE FOR HIS CREATION

We have an unwritten pact to meet and we trust each other. Yes, your writings are to be shared with discrimination. We will guide you as to what and when. When we spoke sometime back about publishing, we *were* speaking of the inner personal things. Universal, eternal, cosmic truth is for all—it belongs to no one and is meant to be shared.

Help Others Expand Their Spiritual Awareness

The reason I came as I did yesterday, Philip, was in response to your question about your spiritual efforts. Also, you recently requested me to come in a dream to clarify. One day I will do this, but not just yet[9]. As your faith grows, such an appearance is possible. I came yesterday, first, because I head up your work. Second, I wanted to encourage you personally. And third, I wanted to make you understand how vital are your writings. It cements our relationship on deeper and deeper levels.

Your writing will go far and touch the eye, ear, and heart of many. Yours is an addition to the world's evolution and revolution. It is one of the ways to help others understand God's providence

---

[9] True to his promise, Saint Germain did eventually appear to me in dreams conveying such profound information and love that I sometimes awoke with tears on my cheeks.

in this age. It will be a body of work studied by many to substantiate the reality of life after death. Its purposes are multiple. But a main purpose is to give such witness to others. Through you, we seek to raise the awareness of many others regarding communication, spirit dynamics, energies, and much more. When others read your writings in their entirety, they will grasp readily the spirit and import of these works. Just know this as you progress.

I stand to your right and my thoughts blend with yours. There is energy all about you. And I want to add that in this state of mind and when you receive for others, you are receiving very clearly. Do not doubt this anymore. As you accept this reality, it is easier and easier for us to tune in and tune you up to increase the clarity of your receiving. We want this greater clarity. While remaining humble is vital, do not apologize in any way for what you receive. Be bold to speak out, and we will be able to come through more clearly. Remember always—the ultimate control is with you.

Awaken to God's Presence within Yourself

For now, our words will almost always be a mixture of giving you higher truth and raising you up in it. We will not always have something philosophically profound to say. We know that you like this most because you are a truth-seeker. But we must concern ourselves with your overall development.

The light which you see just now as you close your eyes is the violet flame of mine. It is *not* mine, but is what I have chosen to come in. I wanted you to see it clearly because it is one sign of my nearness.

There are times when you falter while taking down our dictations. We are in the stream of your thought and *are not* trying to demonstrate our presence by outward signs. It is very normal to look for visible, spiritual manifestations in the form of clairvoyance, clairaudience, or by our usual, easily perceived electrical touch. But we do not constantly seek to display our powers in these ways. Often we do give you outward evidence. And you discern this evidential guidance. But, we are also seeking to raise you to know us by an inner presence as well. This is the age in which our appearance is made known in the heart and mind of man and not so much, as in past ages, by external phenomena. Man must come to realize and awaken to the fact that God is within.

Make Your Spiritual Practices Positive

How do you get better at moving more and more into this thought stream we share? Practice does make perfect. When you come on the foundation of purity and prayer, it is easiest for us to come through. However, we want you to get past all of the sacrificial ideas now. You have done that enough to the negative extreme. It is now time to build up your life force! First, you must accept yourself as a son of the Father! Second, you must claim your inheritance. Third, you must practice it! Out of this most fundamental structure comes the power for thinking positively.

Pray, yes; fulfill spiritual practices, but keep them positive. In practical terms, sacrifice your personal life by attending to all that is needed to fulfill this mission. Stay up late, if absolutely needed, to study, to pray, to serve—but do not suffer anymore in self-denial. Seek with everything you have to achieve the highest and best in this work. Be avaricious for God! We must bring this world back to Him, and to do that is to proclaim our right to do so against all odds.

You often wish you had more energy and physical strength. You are doing fine just as you are. The important thing is to be your own unique self. Our uniqueness is our gift to the world. It is the internal spiritual strength which you possess that is most valuable for our purposes. I tell you no one is stronger or more unstoppable than a man who is on fire for God.

Do not go out of your way any longer to bring suffering onto yourself as a karmic condition or for spiritual advancement. That is a thing of the past for you. Enough is enough. To do it beyond a certain level is to live as if you were still in need of punishment. You must see yourself in the most positive terms, so you can become what you were born to become.

However, if while doing God's will you meet with resistance, if you suffer criticism, if you experience even physical abuse, endure it and it will be used karmically to advance the cause which you serve. This kind of suffering may be unavoidable but it is not self-inflicted. Just remember: if you are going to stand for something, someone may stand against you. And while enduring you will abundantly receive God's grace and be victorious in the end. Proclaim God's right, through you, to become *all* that He created you to be by going forward most joyfully and positively.

Do Not Throw Yourself Off a Cliff to Climb Higher

I reserve my heart's energy in bringing this message through, for I am filled with energy to proclaim this principle. It is time for you to stand and be counted now. Yesterday was yesterday, and today is today! I say, climb the mountain before you. As you do so you will fatigue soon enough. But do not throw yourself down a cliff to pay the price to climb higher! If someone else should throw you down a cliff, that is an obstacle to meet and overcome on the way. Then, rise up, clean off your wounds and go on climbing! This is positive karma.

I touched upon a remembrance in reference to your writings in the past. You often kept your suffering alive in those days. You were surrounded with energies that blocked you and sustained your limitations. By doing so you blocked your own way. You *must not* do that anymore. Remain humble to the fact that God is supreme. But you need to grow in your awareness that God also dwells in *you*. From this reality you can gain rightful self-confidence. If you don't believe in yourself how can God believe in you? Heavenly Father wants all His children to be winners! To do that you must think like a winner! Think only victory! Victory! Victory! Victory!

Reflecting upon those "ancient" writings of yours, in those bitter years of becoming—who authored them, do you think? That you shall know in spirit world. But were they not lengthy receivings? Were you alone in those years? Those works were your connection to heaven in those hours when no one else could help or reach you.

But you were not then where you are now. Now you know your source and guidance! Now there is proof of the origin and the inner working of all of this receiving. Now it is easier and easier to realize that this is all truly happening. You wanted to believe in those days too, but there was little or no way to validate objectively that these were genuine receivings. On the foundation of all of that, you are here today! Congratulations, for not only have you come a long way, but you now know without question that you are in tune!

Your Greatest Fulfillment Is to Help Others Find God

You think of me and my needs because all of this seems to be about you. Well, rest assured that I am fulfilled in helping you. Yes, I have needs, but they are not earthly. I have searched a long time for someone to hear me and the forces I represent clearly. It is gratifying beyond words to be able to come through in this way. I left ego behind eons ago. It doesn't mean I don't feel and think independently, but my needs are one with His. What makes Him happy makes me happy. If by doing this work, I can please Him, then that is enough. I work for the overall evolution of man. And it is only as we raise others to be like ourselves, and thus like Him, that we are fulfilled. You know that in yourself, Philip.

Do you not seek others like yourself who see this work as number one in life's priorities? Does your heart not long for others to hunger enough to seek as you seek and develop as you develop? Wouldn't you welcome such a person? Those with whom you feel closest are those who are willing and desirous to be dedicated for the work itself and not for ego or lesser motives. Keep up your example—it rubs off. Stay above personality, favor no one, favor dedication only! You are being watched and talked about. And we want this, because your dedication to purpose ultimately witnesses to this work more clearly, more loudly than anything you could do personally.

Most people see dedication and admire it. But seldom do they see it apart from ego. Everyone wants something. But to want something because Heavenly Father wants it is the highest motive. It is only in dedication to as lofty a goal as yours that one can come to merge with this awareness. This is most important—*the most important thing in life!* Only in this way does man discover his own divinity and that God is working with him.

Rest and come back. We will wait.

God Is the One True Reality behind Every Form

There are so many things to learn, aren't there? So many object lessons. But these things are seen only by those who have an eye and heart to see. Everywhere we look, we can see God and His will at work. There is nothing in life that can't teach us if we seek oneness with Him. Who is He anyway? I often use the words "it is so simple" to drive home a point. Because life *is* simple! Remove all of today's unnecessary modern contrivances, and you have the world as He intended. That is not to say the modern world with its sophisticated inventions is evil. But instead of being grateful and realizing the eternal force behind such genius, man marvels at the invention and *his* inventiveness and misses the true reality behind all life. This is a great, great sadness to the Creator. To give and give and yet be ignored is too much for anyone.

Remove yourself from the world and go back to simplicity. If you want a meaningful day, spend it gazing upon and studying a flower. Put all other earthly cares and distractions aside. Don't try to be philosophical or think highly of yourself, but let life from one flower flow to you and then grasp its greatness and its true origin! In one flower is *all* the truth of life. Here is God in earthly solid form!

It is very sad that man sees only the form and not the Creator behind the form. It is by our daily interaction with creation, including other human beings, that we are to realize the Author behind all of life.

All forms in this physical world are an outward manifestation of the inner divine intelligence and love of God. If we carefully study life around us, we can easily discern that there is a beautiful, intelligent, caring, highly organized, just, and loving Being who brought all of life into existence.

All is a gift of God which He unselfishly shares with us. He is no Father who simply wants worship. What is worship after all? Is it not our genuine expression of love and gratitude to the Parent who gave us life? Is this so wrong? Should we not be grateful and express our worship of God—at least by an expression of thanks within our hearts? Our love is all that He desires from us. Nothing more! He owns everything, so there is nothing we can give to Him that is not already His. The only thing we can give to Him that He does not own is our love.

Love is not a bouquet of flowers, or an altar covered with fine linen and burning candles. It is not money. Love is what we feel in our hearts when we are humble and grateful to God or anyone. And all outward efforts to give love are but forms through which to demonstrate or express our love. But they are not the love itself.

Out of Innocent Love God Created All for All

Because God is love He knows nothing but giving. It is not in His nature to withhold love any more than water can exist without wetness or light without heat or night without day. God created everything for us. All is given freely to man.

It is hard for materialistic man to see this reality. It is hard for man who always seeks a return for his investment to believe God wouldn't. They fail to see LOVE. Love in its highest expression escapes them. And so He goes on looking and looking for those who truly love and appreciate love for love's sake, nothing more, nothing less!

Behind each flower is an energy that keeps it sustained, alive, vital. That energy is unseen by unevolved man. Behind every form is this Life Force, more real, definitely transcendent, and containing absolute love. God is behind every form. Only when man is raised back to Eden, can he begin to know.

Still, without ceasing, this Force does not relinquish its purpose. It pours forth tirelessly and returns to its source. God basks in the beauty of all that He has made out of Himself, with few to share His love or His joy in all of this.

There is a revolution going on—it cannot be stopped. And it shall have its way. This love, and He as its origin and He behind all forms, even man, will be clearly known. It is that time. He has advanced forward minute by minute through those whom He has ordained to win the war of love. He is the creator and possessor of all love. He is winning step by step with love. The cumulative sowing is springing forth in the fields of history at this moment, and the earth shall be overrun with this abundance. It cannot, will not, be stopped. Love is on a rampage, growing like energy out of control, and will leave no one untouched in its path as it spreads, thank God, prolifically everywhere.

"My word shall not go forth unfruitful. *All* that I have prophesied and promised will be fulfilled!"

For one to come through this way on this topic which is *the* topic of topics, one must have been there, or be on the way. This has been the search for those prepared for this day to be used by Him for the highest truth and the highest love. Cultivation of such an age with such souls has taken eons. But the hybrid is here now! The crop is waiting to be harvested. And those who are ready and waiting will know and respond. This is just the beginning.

Rest and continue your day. We will be with you every minute as you seek to fulfill this divine call.

Yours always in Him,

Saint Germain and Band

5:44 A.M.
March 20, 1988
West Grove, Pennsylvania

Chapter Twenty-Eight

Helping Others: The Key To Your Growth

There should be no doubt that I am here *and* near. I am flowing in the stream of your conscious and subconscious thoughts. As I do so, you pick them up as your own unless you distance yourself from them and thereby discern or differentiate. Then you can make a distinction between the two voices.

Each Person Develops Spiritually at His Own Pace

It is a grand day. And we were so very pleased with your obedience this morning to allow us to come through. You should not compare yourself to another. Each unfolds according to his particular design of being and mission. Do not look down on others either, for if they are bringing even one soul closer to God then they are serving the over-all evolution of man and the cosmic higher purpose. God is wise to make use of the imperfect for by doing so He not only brings others closer to Him but raises the imperfect to perfection at the same time. This is a part of His grand scheme.

Your work is moving along well. Keep it simple still and allow each of those who follows you to move forward at his individual pace. Be sensitive to this and simply encourage each one where he is today. I try to do that from this side through their guides. And to some, as you have already discovered, I come directly. Teach them what you were taught this morning about always refueling daily with the energy of God. This is more central to their existence than any other thing you can teach. Do teach it.

As you turn the page we want to say you *are* turning a new page of life. And while appearances may be deceptive there is change and progress. You will look back on these times and forget the fatigue and frustrations. You will remember the meaningfulness of pioneering in new lands and crossing spiritual landmarks in the forward movement. We too are pushed by heaven's demand. We feel the pressure too and pass it on to you. Because the end is glorious we do not regret this pressure.

Love Others According to Their Individual Needs

And to what purpose are you moving forward? It is not for the structure of an institution or for buildings and their adoration. It is not for the moneys collected and used to live. You are moving forward by helping others for the purpose of helping others. Forget numbers and place the emphasis upon the quality of love among you. Help people find themselves in God. Use your teaching and encouragement for meditation and spiritual awakening on every level to enhance the individual awareness and life, that through this means they can come closer to, and experience more and more of Him. Keep your meditation upon this and this alone and you will be successful beyond words.

Reach out to each soul by putting yourself in his place, realizing his needs, and loving him accordingly. Love is not sentimentality or mere warm physical contact. Love is caring for someone according to their individual needs. All the sentiment and all the physical touching will not help without knowing and meeting needs. This approach is a safeguard against sameness in love. Love in general, yes, but love specifically, too. Take the time, make the time to love individually. Individual caring will go far in cementing others to your work. If people feel personally loved they will gravitate toward the center of the Source of such love. Do all of this and you can't help but be successful!

We do not want to put words out on paper for words' sake. No, we want quality in writing. We want to leave you and the future with information that hits the mark and makes a deep and lasting impression. So today we leave off here to let the reader explore deeply and fully the dictates of true love, the demands of truly loving.

In true love,

Saint Germain

6:10 A.M.
April 10, 1988
West Grove, Pennsylvania

CHAPTER TWENTY-NINE

LOVE IN ACTION

Love in action will begin the process of healing. Love, when given completely, draws the Spirit of God in to stabilize, to heal, to raise the mind. You see, it is not love alone in human relations that maintains the equilibrium. It is love between humans, when elevated to a self-sacrificing level, that draws out of oneself the spirit of God that is already present in the human soul. This higher love takes over and re-creates a higher and new relationship.

Release Yourself from Yourself To Find Yourself

Often humans in their present condition cannot give up their negative feelings, but seek retaliation or hold grudges. This state of mind damages the soul. Since in his present state man does not *naturally* sacrifice his negative feelings, he must do it *deliberately*. He must walk through the pain of the grudge within himself to achieve the freedom, glory, and godly love of the higher self. Few people discover this because they are afraid they might lose something by giving up their grudges, their hurts, their angers. So long have they identified with these inner turmoils that they are not happy unless they express them. But it is not true happiness, for negativity always begets negativity. Few have released themselves of themselves to find their higher self in God.

Jesus has taught us to choose the path of God: to love sacrificially, sacrificing our own personal feelings to love as God loves. God wants to love through us, you see. God literally wants to reach out His arms through our arms and embrace His children. He wants to impart a holy kiss upon the cheek of each of His children. He wants and needs to do this through mankind. When He can do this universally and cosmically, He will be dwelling fully among mankind. As it is written, "His dwelling place is among men."

While man ambitiously pursues earthly goals he misses his divine reality, his divine calling. Then when he achieves it all, he wonders why he is still unfulfilled, unhappy and often at odds with others, including those closest to him.

Even those who call themselves religious often do not truly, truly understand God's goal for their life. They think: mission, mission, mission. And if they are successful in landing a niche or place in life and hold a title in some ecclesiastical institution, they think themselves devout, religious, and holy!

You Are Free When God Fully Dwells in You

Fulfillment in life is the indwelling of God totally within man so that man is completely animated by His energy, His spirit, His heart. This is not poetry; this is not philosophy; this is not good feelings. This is to be the true reality of man on earth. Man is the church; man is the temple; man is the shrine; man is the vessel— man, man, man! We cannot make this clear enough. We cannot say it enough.

Jesus taught to seek first the Kingdom of Heaven. And he said the Kingdom was within. It *is* within! Man should seek to free himself of all impurities, to clear the passageway for God to make His full entrance, His complete appearance within man. Man should seek to empty himself of self and to ask the Father to help him do that—allowing a totally cleared, holy space for God to live.

We should not seek ritual, religion, or philosophy to enjoy its outward feelings or appearances. Rather, we need to know that *we* are the object of His love and that we are truly incomplete without this love's filling us to maximum capacity. We must long for this love, His presence within us, so totally, so completely, that it actually happens. When we break through the barriers of our hearts and open wide our minds and clear out the self, give up the self for a greater, God-enhanced self, we are free, truly free.

In man's freedom to use his own initiative, it is within his power to welcome God in, to ask Him to take over completely. This is the right use of free will. And when a man's mind is elevated to this understanding, he will stop abusing the use of his free will and allow God's takeover. God did not expect man to be otherwise, for He created him with potential to be God's image and likeness. God thought man would do so, for He Himself gave up Self to create man to love and be with man. Surely man would do the same for Him. But, because he did not and has not, few have risen to the level of really understanding what life is all about. The power of life lies within man, insofar as God dwells fully therein.

Great Is He Who Is a Master of Love

Therefore, go with God. Go against your tendency to deny others your love; embrace them against the tide of your own inclination to reject. And while they may not return the same or even understand, life will bless you. And God will enter into you more and more fully.

What the world needs are a few such people, those who care

only to see God fully in each person. As leaven in bread, such love multiplies. This and all the above is precisely what your life and work is about.

Focus your inner sight upon the ever-present Father. See Him go before you in all circumstances. And trust Him completely as you express love in action, to come through you and heal you of all illnesses of the mind, the heart, and the body. This and this alone is truly living and true life. Go forth and see.

There are many high-realm forces gathered around you just now. They stand seeking your elevation into their society of love. Self-mastery is the center of their life—and where else but in love? They have sought the Christ example as their point of emulation. They saw the reality to which God is calling *all* of us. They answered the call, and practiced the continued presence of God. While on earth they were masked in many diverse and often humble positions. But quietly, hidden away from the world, they practiced the art of loving Him and opening to Him. When they came to this side they were indeed elevated, full bearers of His heart. That work is yet to run its course. Today they, like myself, seek to traverse the final miles to Him. For this reason we are with you and with those whom you call your brothers and sisters in spirit.

We are and will continually stand guard these final days on earth. This is the day of the conclusion of His will on earth. Stick to the path and you will help many to see and to live this realization.

Glory to God in man! Glory to God in the highest! Bless His holy Name!

We are yours in His service,

Saint Germain and All

8:00 A.M.
April 20, 1988
Riverdale, Maryland

CHAPTER THIRTY

THE REALITY OF GOD'S LOVE

The problems of life are multiple and complex. The solutions are simple. The origin of life is also the One who contains the answers to life. It is man without truth who has turned the world of thought into a quagmire of confusion.

Seeking for Ultimate Truth Leads to Freedom

The Author of life is pure love and is desirous of giving and receiving love. Return to this simple truth and you can re-establish stability within yourself. Surrounding each lost, ignorant soul are ideas and concepts of how life is and should be. And these ideas and concepts are a mixture of truth and falsehood in varying degrees. Some people's thoughts contain greater truth and less falsehood. And conversely, other people's thoughts are filled with greater falsehood and less truth. And there are all shades in between.

Most struggle between these two extremes within the mind. And we suffer as victims of our own thoughts. This is *not* figurative, but absolutely real in the everyday existence of *all* people. Therefore, only as man seeks and lives truth—undeniable, unchanging, eternal, empirical truth—does he find hope and freedom. We may continue to delude ourselves by thinking otherwise. As we have told you before: truth is truth and it remains forever. In the spirit world there can be no argument or opinions, for in the highest of realms only the truth is known. Here only the truth exists—it is not arguable!

Only on earth, where ultimate reality is hidden behind material existence and man's blindness, is truth questioned. All realms except the highest are resultant from the falsehood and partial truths existing on earth. So these realms cannot be said to be pure or absolute realms. The people are not evil in the classical sense, but are still in lesser truth and are therefore somewhat dissatisfied, yearning and needing to go higher.

Because in all realms where there is reasonable understanding there is also light, we can see the Source of that light and can experience its effect upon our minds and hearts. This experience causes us to want to be as close as possible to the light so that our minds and hearts are maximally imbued with His presence. In the highest realms of the spirit world, no longer is the light just outside of us but we experience it shining brightly within. No longer is there distance between us and our Beloved. In these realms God and we are one.

You Will Find Your Eternal Parents in God

On earth children want to be as close to the *center* of life as possible. Their parents' love and guidance draws them to the core of the family—the parents. It is natural. And in the greatest innocence there is the greatest purity and the greatest attraction to pure, parental love. So compelling is this love that we cannot help ourselves. This love is food to the spirit. Nowhere else can we go to secure it as we can from our parents. For this reason we will search our entire life to find parental love if we have been given less than ideal parents. It is parental love that fills a soul in its beginning journey on earth. This is God's original intention.

Where there are most ideal parents—made ideal by love and wisdom—there you will find an ideal child and an ideal family comprising ideal children. This is the working model of heaven in the spirit world: we are children of the Father. It is so throughout eternity. We are naturally and necessarily drawn to Him to complete our life. Without Him life cannot be completed. This is fact well seen and understood in spirit. We do not argue that point in the realms of light. We spend our energies appreciating His beneficent parental love pouring through and around us. We seek to find the shortest route to come closer and closer to Him.

He is not a matter of belief or faith in the realms of light. He is fact to be seen everywhere! This fact is one of the first enormous realities awakening souls realize when they arrive in our world. This fact alone brings remorse to the newly emerging spirit. His regret lies in that had he known without question—as he does now upon his arrival—God's unarguable reality, he would have spent his earthly life so differently. This is regret of the deepest kind.

But we are not condemned. Those who serve the newly arrived soul quickly go about the business of teaching their new charge how now to use energy constructively, to enhance his awareness of God in our midst, and to learn and apply ways of growing ever closer to the eternal Parent.

Rearrange Your Priorities to Fulfill Your Divine Purpose

When life is seen from this perspective, a thousand unnecessary thoughts fall away from our minds. Instead, we want to "be about our Father's business!" We can more easily arrange our priorities in life and place emphasis upon the fundamental reality. This is the beginning of true and complete healing. Life in its cause and effect when viewed from this perspective is simple.

This does not mean that our problems just fall away as if by some kind of religious magic. But it does mean that by seeking Him first we can be helped in this bond, and He can closely guide us and help us eliminate mental encumbrances more easily and more quickly. Our burden is lifted and made lighter by knowing He is there. Again, we speak literally, not figuratively!

Even this moment as you read these words, does it dawn within your mind how uplifting they are for you? Think of this reality and then think of your unfolding day. Will you go on centering your existence upon the mundane? If He exists, if there is a Creator and First Cause, isn't this vital to your life's journey? Think upon this reality and see if in some way you can today discover some manifest experience that tells you that our words are true.

You are upon your life's journey now. Its beginning is on earth but its greater portion is in spirit. We ask you only to think upon this idea for your life today. Include its *possibility* if you have not in the past.

Life's Ultimate Goal Is to Be Love Incarnate

We return to speak of the highest realms: only pure love may enter into these realms. Falsehood and truth do not co-exist in the highest of highest realms where in all the cosmos He dwells most completely. Access to these climes is made possible only as one is as the Father is: love and truth itself. To dwell here is to dwell at the absolute center of love. There can be nothing but absolute pure love. Those who dwell here must and do think as He thinks, and feel as He feels. They are one with Him and have but one wish and will: to be an extension of Him and to parent mankind, to bring His love and concern to others, to bring them closer and closer to Him! They know there is no higher purpose for which to exist than God's will. In this sense they are He in finite form. And they come to other humans to make them ultimately Him in finite form. They are married—wed—to God by the penetration of His love into their hearts. They are His bride and they are one! As brides they receive His love internally and return His love by affection and service. Not servitude but rather devotion and dedication demonstrate their love for Him.

From these elevated souls of pure love and pure light wed to God the Father has created a kind of parenthood to draw his children to Him. And so it has been in human history that these beings of light have descended time and again to earth and the lesser realms of spirit to teach and cajole and draw His creation ever closer and closer to Him!

There is no one who is not a target of His love. There are none who will ultimately escape this reality. He has used endless means and ways to make this grand appeal to mankind. He has used every possible good and loving means to awaken us. And this work continues to this day. And shall continue until all is fulfilled.

Peace will come to the valley of your soul as you ponder and meditate upon our imparted words written here. It is our highest reason to come to earth. All other words, phenomena, and themes are for this one purpose. We can speak no higher. There is no topic equal to or more important than God's existence and God's love. We know factually—not by faith or belief but by direct experience through keen awareness—that this of which we speak is true. Whoever hears it with their heart will know it is true also.

May your life be made happier and more fulfilled by our words. It is our earnest desire and prayer that you realize the truth and value of this writing.

In His Name who is God, Lord, Father and Parent of all, we close.

Saint Germain and Band

5:05 A.M.
September 30, 1988
Los Gatos, California

Historical Information on Saint Germain

The Count of Saint-Germain, by Isabel Cooper-Oakley, Rudolph Steiner Publications, Blauvelt, New York, 1970

The Most Holy Trinosophia, of the Comte de St.-Germain, Introduction and Commentary by Manly P. Hall, The Philosophical Research Society, Inc., Los Angeles, CA, 1983

Association for Internal Mastery, Inc.
also known as
AIM or AIM, Inc.

To learn more about AIM and its outreach programs you may contact the Burleys at the following addresses:

AIM, Inc.
Attn: Philip and Vivien Burley
P.O. Box 14196, Scottsdale, AZ 85267-4196

Fax: 602-483-0546
E-mail: aimhdqts@aol.com

Please write to us if you are interested in the following:

- a private spiritual consultation
- AIM meditation classes
- AIM meditation tapes
- AIM - Universal Healing Circle
- being placed on the AIM mailing list
- AIM catalog of publications, audio tapes and CD's

Make sure to clearly print your name, address, and fax or Internet number.

AIM has also published *A Wanderer in the Spirit Lands*, by Franchezzo, transcribed by A. Farnese, © 1993, foreword by Philip Burley. Available through AIM Publishers or bookstores throughout America.

Philip and Vivien welcome all letters, comments and inquiries.